POLITICAL SOUND BITES OF A CONCERNED NIGERIAN

Reflections on value-based leadership and citizenship

Mfon O. Bassey

ISBN: 978-978-989-202-0

DEDICATION

This book is dedicated to all true patriots.

TABLE OF CONTENT

Foreword

I have always described the internet as a separate planet - the tenth if you may. Although peopled by the same humans that populate the earth; yet feels like man's frequent shuttles to outer space. We have become so used to the virtual world that we imagine it as an alternate universe. It is a place you can connect with Dangote or insult Bill Gates and life goes on.

The internet brought us Facebook. Like earth, the social media bears so much resemblance with continents and countries for that matter. Facebook in particular being the most used virtual medium in Nigeria has afforded countless of millions of Nigerians the opportunity to share orientation, meet, forge relationships and in some cases become family.

One of such persons is Mfon. His uncanny way of piecing his thoughts together stands him head and shoulders above his peers as a giant of thought and process. His stubborn insistence on articulating and sharing his muse and doing so consistently shows him off as a man in charge of his being.

You cannot doubt the immense scholarship he puts in his articles, neither can you fault his deep patriotism even where he appears to stand alone on issues.

It is the above qualities that invited my friendship and we haven't looked back. He is a frequent contributor to our modest news website - Politicos.ng where he shares his nationalistic interventions with elan.

So, when I was given the chance to burrow through this work, I took it as an honor rather than a task. Reading through confirms the redoubtable Nigerian champion of the first order he is and will always be.

This book is not intimidated by the many side distractions that is common in a world that is weary of state and it's actors. On the contrary, 'Political Sound Bites of a Concerned Nigerian' reveals in very clear form - nuggets of why and how our country deserves the mountain top in spite of being rooted in clay like the proverbial giant.

The author does not just bemoan our woes, rather he shares years of thinking, studying, understanding and comparing precepts, concepts and theories of what can work for us to make better progress economically, socially and politically.

Mfon's unimpeachable character, principles, values and love for country runs through and deep in all the lines, pages and chapters such that you cannot but read to the end.

This work gives palpable hope that Nigeria's future is assured in spite of occasional hiccups. For like me, the book reveals that our challenges are man-made as such can be resolved by man if we put our hands on the plough and not look back.

Hear him: "Like other noble professions, have we made any attempt to define the philosophy that should underpin politics in this country? What I'm saying is; upon which philosophy is politics built in this country? Is it built on the philosophy of selfless service to humanity and social justice or is it built on the philosophy of election violence and rigging, stealing, lying, plunder, power shift and rotation, mediocrity, ethnicity, gangsterism, lawlessness, materialism, greed, sybaritism and other negative vices one can think of?"

This is the kind of poser that jogs Mfon. It is others like this that underscored his determination to complete this work.

I can say straight away that what you have in your hands is a practical political science text; guide to the right politics in Nigeria and how Nigeria can attain faster development.

The lucid and itemized manner the book is presented makes for easy reading. It joggles your thought when his story bounces off from sociology, to philosophy, economics and history.

Here is a complete compendium for anyone who truly desires politics of the big picture, the deliverables and a socially conscious citizenry.

This book does not have space for indolence or quick fixes. Instead, it is filled with pages of ways and means, hope for the weary, manual for the young and tools for the prepared.

This book will generate further discussions. Mfon, the engineer who provides business solutions joins other professionals who are elated by the enriching of minds. It is not surprising that his first book goes above and beyond to proffer practical solutions to governance and citizenship challenges. May the disagreements and arguments that will naturally follow this work produce another one.

Uche Nnadozie

INTRODUCTION

As far back as the Guardian of Tuesday July 16, 2013 page 11, Isaac Taiwo had reported that, 'former Secretary-General of the Commonwealth, Chief Emeka Anyaoku, has expressed worry and fear over the state of the Nigerian nation. To him, the country is facing crisis "while our leaders and elites are living in denial of those facts"'. This presupposes that the way forward is not denial but facing up to the problems so as to fix them.

The state of the Nigerian nation, truth be told, is troubling but the good news is that it is not beyond repairs. This is because, fortunately for us, Nigeria's problems are man-made and can therefore be undone by man, in this case, Nigerians - me and you.

The 200 sound bites contained in this book are nuggets, questions and observations I made and updated over an extended period which are still pertinent and can be framed for debates to get more insightful outlooks. Soundbite number 43 made this reference to its inspiration, quote: "This nugget was informed by the write up of a popular newspaper columnist with a popular Nigerian newspaper who referred to (then) Vice President Namadi Sambo as a northern politician, "who refused to provide a rallying point for an agitated north". The columnist found himself on the wrong foot when I reached out to him and asked him "what ails the northern part of Nigeria that doesn't ail the south and why Vice President Namadi Sambo should provide a rallying point for an agitated north instead of providing a rallying point for an agitated nation?"

They are arranged in chapters according to the issues they address in politics and society. The chapter titles which represent positive expectations are 1. Integrity in Leadership 2. Leadership Excellence 3. Institutional Integrity 4. Quality Citizenship 5. Embrace Positive 6. Right Orientation 7. Common Sense Issues 8. Economic Matters, and 9. The Nigeria of my Dream.

The book identifies poor leadership, positive values deficiency, wrong orientation, greed, sentiments, impunity and most especially official corruption and indiscipline among the leadership and the led - with the leadership getting most of the knocks - as the cause of most of our woes. This is against the notion in some quarters (which are reasonable arguments in their own rights) that Nigeria's problem is its governance structure and that if we go back to regional arrangements, fiscal federalism, parliamentary system of government and a cocktail of other prescriptions, Nigeria will be restored.

In spite of the system we have or the one we choose to adopt, I am convinced that strict adherence to rules, regulations and discipline is non-negotiable and will always be the way forward.

My views presented here are based on common sense. A government, whether parliamentary or presidential should enforce its laws and uphold discipline. I also believe that if we imbibe the virtues of Section 23 of the 1999 constitution as amended which states that, "The national ethics shall be Discipline, Integrity, Dignity of Labor, Social Justice, Religious Tolerance, Self-reliance and Patriotism", we will turn the corner.

GRAB A COPY, Relax, read, comprehend and act right. God bless Nigeria, Long live Africa!

CHAPTER ONE

Integrity in Leadership

1.	A leader must have (or know) what he is living to die for if he must make a difference. While a leader, like any other human being is not expected to offer his head to the guillotine or be careless about his safety and security; there must be an ideal, whose pursuit or whose defense, he concedes might cost him his life. If there is no worthy ideal you are willing to pay the supreme sacrifice or ultimate prize for, then you are not a leader.

2.	Our development vocabulary should include integrity and honesty in public life as a primary requirement for development.

3.	Leaders work for the people; they don't steal from them – they rather give to them. Band of people who are using government offices to feather their nest are not leaders but bandits.

4.	What is your mission in politics? What's your reason for joining politics? Many Nigerian politicians are in politics to serve. Yes, to serve themselves and their families. Ask the politician who come seeking for votes why she joined politics; her mission in politics and how she envisions achieving it.

5.	The politics of most Nigerian politicians is based on the fantasies of becoming important persons driven in convoys with ambulance like sirens and the reveries of being pampered, getting first class treatments, having their pictures in institutions and public places, being cheered, amassing wealth and living the good life. It is not based on selfless sacrificial service aimed at adding value to the society and making people's lot better. If it did, their disproportionate logic defying salaries and allowances or desperation for power which leads to electoral violence and election rigging will not be a recurring decimal here. The enormous and important duties, responsibilities and demands of their offices are completely lost on them.

6.   Most leadership cohorts in African countries like Nigeria, South Sudan and others see power as an instrument for resource expropriation for their own personal benefits rather than a tool for resource exploitation for their people's benefit. That's why there is so much underdevelopment and strife in sub Saharan Africa where majority of their undernourished and poorly educated people live in squalor and conflicts in such places as Nigeria, South Sudan, Central Africa Republic etc. Places where their gullible people – who can't think straight because short term mentality, poverty, greed, sentiments and prejudices have sapped their capacity to do so – are used as cannon fodders by their malevolent and sybaritic elites to achieve their selfish goals.

7.   Our leaders should concentrate on leaving legacies that will outlive them, instead of the present quest for the primitive accumulation of material wealth by using public offices to advance personal gains. This makes the primary activities of these leaders geared towards achieving their selfish interests and not the public interest. That is why policies, programmes and projects don't succeed as publicized.

8.   The concept of leadership is that of sacrifice. A leader's vision is for a better life for all and he is willing to make the necessary sacrifices to ensure that he achieves it even at a personal cost. He is happy when people are happy, successful and prosperous. He is sad when people are sad, struggling, sick, unhealthy, unsuccessful and poor. Therefore, there is no place for jealously or competition with people in the heart of a leader. He wants to add value to people's life. He is rather unhappy when people are being oppressed. If he has anything against anyone, it is oppression. He fights injustice and cheating. He does so compassionately, with a view to correcting and restoring the offender. He is very much concerned about peoples' welfare and well-being and therefore will not take what belongs to the people: even a penny. He might be a person of excellence and quality but he is not extravagant and flamboyant. He cuts his suit according to his cloth and doesn't engage in ostentations that might lead him to become dubious and steal. He has rectitude and does not live beyond his means. He is a very aware person; conscious of setting a good example for others to follow. Therefore, he disciplines and denies himself pleasures that may lead to harmful and addictive habits. He is concerned about the poor and weak; the need to protect them from the rich, strong and wicked. He is concerned about the rich and wealthy; the need to protect them from the poor, weak and wicked.

9.   If we must develop and build a healthy and prosperous nation, there are things which we MUST do. We can't run away from them. We can pretend all we can, we can sermonize all we can but if we don't do them or change them, we are going nowhere. One of such things is

the practice by politicians and civil servants whereby they distribute government contracts among themselves. It is said that every contract belongs to someone in Nigeria. A minister, a permanent secretary, a director, a director-general, an executive secretary, members of the board of agencies and parastatals. This is really ludicrous as much as it is mind boggling to a rational adult that contract belongs to individuals not the Nigerian state. These same people will climb the rostrum and sermonize on change, transformation and development. In any case, the incontrovertible fact is that if we don't change or do the right thing, we are going nowhere to happen; we will just be chasing shadows!

10.   We need to institutionalize procedures for transparent governance founded on the rule of law whose observance should be strictly adhered to and enforced. We should institutionalize transparency and accountability. Unfortunately, instead of our informed and educated elites questioning wrong actions of the government and demanding for transparency and accountability as a matter of principle, conviction and values; they line up with bowls crooning before political office holders for money, contracts, appointments and favors. Threatening or harassing the government comes when some are left out or ignored in the sharing of bounties. That is, our elites are pursuing contracts, appointments and favors; there is no demand for transparency and accountability from their peers or friends in government by them except when they are disgruntled or when there is a conflict of interest and this is very wrong.

11.	We need to save ourselves from ourselves by reaching deep into our humanity to find the love, empathy, courage and strength to act with dignity and do the right thing at all times. We need to find the resolve, character and discipline to make the necessary sacrifices for national greatness. The word patriotism has lost its significance, relevance, potency and meaning in contemporary Nigeria. The best word for the people and leaders that can convey the enormity of citizen duties and responsibilities needed to get Nigeria out of the woods of indiscipline, mediocrity, impunity et al and into the right track of discipline, excellence, rule of law and other good virtues is selfless sacrificial service. We have work to do here. We have to work twice (or more) as hard as citizens of any other nation on earth to recover the lost glory of our fatherland and restore its pride. We cannot run away from selfless sacrificial service (triple S or 3S). There is no country in the world that is progressing today which does not boast of an epoch where selfless sacrificial leadership cohorts represented by a rallying person say a Lee Kwan Yew for Singapore, a Winston Churchill for Britain, an Abraham Lincoln for U.S., a Nelson Mandela for South Africa etc. burst into the scene and gave up their privileges to serve their people and mobilize them for national greatness. This is what we need in Nigeria, a leadership cohort who will offer selfless sacrificial service.

12.	We need to train leaders to be economically independent, to view politics as a place to spend (if you have money) and or serve (if you don't have money to contribute). We need to raise people we can give a private or public office to and be sure they will never steal; use it to pursue personal goals and selfish interests or give room for their subordinates to do so.

13.   In our society, some people see stealing corporate or company money and government funds as smart ways or means of advancing in life financially and economically. Business owners and managers know how shrewd they have to be and the kind of financial controls and security measures they have to put in place to protect, secure and possibly prevent their business assets such as cash, goods or inventory, equipment etcetera from being stolen by dishonest employees. Even at that, some employees despite the barriers still invent ways and means of stealing from their employers (public or private). What then do you think will happen when such employees who steals from their employers, become politicians and find themselves in government houses or public offices through our might is right and the end justifies the means electoral process? What will happen when they find themselves in government offices where the bar against stealing is very low - and the amount to be stolen very high - because the eagle eyes (law enforcement agencies and whistle blowers encouraged by a robust witness protection system) that are supposed to monitor them are either blind, sleeping or can be easily compromised? What will happen when they go into public offices where safeguards are inadequate and financial controls very weak or non-existent? What will happen where the codes of transparency and accountability in governance and administration are observed in the breach? What will happen where no one is questioned after stealing and using the proceeds to build or buy big mansions, marry more wives, buy posh cars and live evidently beyond his means with swagger? What will

happen in institutions where these individuals with itchy fingers preside over and are guardians of its funds? The answer is despoliation and grand larceny.

That is why to avoid these scenarios, leaders are meant to be proven men of integrity. To achieve this, the constitution specifies or prescribes the qualities and the kind of people who should qualify to aspire for public offices. The constitution even goes as far as barring people with a record of conviction from public offices. Also, would be leaders are supposed to be thoroughly screened, scrutinized and vetted to ensure that they are not susceptible to stealing or abusing their offices. However, what is the status of leadership vetting in Nigeria today? Individuals even win elections while they are under investigation for corruption or in prison custody. Unethical businessmen, drug barons and smugglers addicted to quick money are not left out. Moreover, can politicians who rig, bribe and instigate violence to win elections have the integrity to lead? The riposte is no! If we must call a spade, a spade; anyone who engages in election rigging and other forms of electoral malpractices, whether he or she eventually loses or wins – and become a president, senator, honorable member, governor, state legislator, local government chairman, councilor or any other electoral office in non-governmental organisations, associations, unions and bodies –is a criminal; short and simple. The pervasiveness of election rigging and other electoral malpractices in Nigeria therefore is a testimony to the kind of people who have been making their way into leadership positions since 1999 and what they have done to the public till. A society whose people don't care about who their leaders really are, and are lackadaisical about ascertaining the genuineness, quality, true character and real motive of their leaders in favor of sentiments, gossips and baseless rumors will experience 'kwashiorkored' (stunted) development and growth. The solution is to go back to the basic rudiments of leadership selection and recruitment supported by the spirit and letters of our laws.

14.   We need to fix stipends people can earn in politics doing leg works as volunteers instead of doling out huge sums to campaign staff and crowd organizers. How are these funds recouped? Public offices and political appointments should not be seen to confer economic advantages.

15.   If I may ask, the disease and the symptom, which one is worse? I don't think it will take much time for anyone to arrive at an answer because it is common knowledge that the disease is worse than the symptom. This common agreement is based on the fact that the disease gives rise to the symptom - without the disease, there will be no symptom. Cure the disease and the symptom will disappear; treat the symptom and it might disappear temporarily only to relapse with full force and sometimes with devastating consequences. It is very heartwarming how Nigerians have risen in indignation and with one voice against the menace of Boko Haram. It must however be noted that politicians who rig elections and pilfer the public till are worse than Boko Haram. This is because they are the disease while Boko Haram is the symptom. The insidious acts of election rigging and diversion of public funds into private pockets through the award of phony and inflated contracts etc. are destructive.

It is these acts that create the conditions and fertile ground for Boko Haram and other anti-social groups and activities to flourish. Our condemnation of the fly which Boko Haram constitutes in our ointment is okay. Our support for the imposition of state of emergency in affected states is in line with our desire for order, security and development. However, if we approach the issues of election rigging and official stealing (we see politicians and public officials live 'far beyond their means but our internal alarm doesn't go off) with the same outrage, indignation and urgency with which we respond to the threat of Boko Haram; defeating Boko Haram, the symptom, will then be easier because we are also dealing with or fighting the disease. Having said that, we might ultimately defeat Boko Haram, but it if we don't exorcise corruption from the body polity, it will be a matter of time before another sinister symptom rears its ugly head from nowhere.

16.   Nigerian politicians who are producing average results when what the country needs is extra ordinary results are not doing so because they are dumb or unintelligent. Just spend time with any of them and you will realize that they are very smart and brilliant. The poor results are because of a virulent strain and malignant kind of selfishness which manifest in greed, excessive and extreme remuneration, crass materialism, ostentation, opulent and lavish lifestyles in a country;

- With a world record 10.5 million out of school children in 2013 according to UNESCO. It should be noted that in 2008, the figure was 10million.
- With a housing deficit of 25million.

- With the highest number of maternal mortalities – 563 out of 100,000(2014).
- Where 112 million out of its 160million people are living below the poverty line of $1 per day. (70% of 160million translate into 112 million people).
- Where 30 million Nigerians defecate openly according to the UN. (I did not know the meaning of open defecation until I witnessed it in a certain community, I went to manage a project where there are waste dumps scattered in several locations inside the community. Meanwhile, children go to these dumpsites to defecate in the open every day. Probably adults go there in the night but I wouldn't know.

It was indeed very shocking to me that such an existence can be going on in a community that is a local government headquarters where there are health inspectors who draw salaries every month. I wondered what political leaders in these areas are thinking. What does it take to teach or help people dig pit toilets and keep it clean if they can't afford water closets?)

- Where 75million people are living in darkness.
- Ranked 15 out of 177 nations in the failed state index (2009). Failed state index is published by Fund for Peace and the magazine, Foreign Policy.
- Ranked 98th out of 104 in the 2009 Legatum Prosperity Index

- Ranked 158th out of 182 countries under the Human Development Index (2009) with a score of 0.511.
- Where in the global report on health of children statistics released by UNICEF in 2009, it was one of the two African nations listed among twenty countries responsible for 80% of malnutrition in children in the world. The indices include 14% low birth weight, 13% exclusive breastfeeding, 14% wasting, 43% stunting and 27% underweight.
- And many other damning indices...

These politicians deploy their intellect very well when it comes to getting something for themselves. The average Nigerian politician will whine, sulk and can set their local governments, their states and even the nation on fire when it comes to achieving their selfish personal goals.

However, they will not heat up the polity or raise a whimper when money for building a road is diverted or the contract inflated. When it comes to thinking for Nigerians, they are very loose and sloppy. They are also slow and inefficient in execution when crumbs are approved. This can be exemplified in 25% for capital projects which will benefit 99% of Nigerians being implemented 55% or 65%. Meanwhile, the 75% for recurrent expenditure which directly benefit 1% of Nigerians is implemented 100%. Is it not a paradox that 1% of Nigerians who receive 75% to oversee the implementation of 25% for 99% of Nigerians can only achieve between 55% and 65% implantation after drawing 100% in full as emoluments? This indeed is an indictment on the political class. They need to take a good look at themselves and change.

17.	The leadership cohort that will transform Nigeria must take an oath to make money by honest means and not by dishonest means. They should be sold to the fact that life is about leaving good and positive legacies. A businessman might be lucky to leave a legacy of riches by making money through dishonest means but no political leadership can make a difference if they are not committed to making money by honest means.

18.	The stated intention of Nigerian politicians in seeking for votes is highly commoditized. They promise the same things in the same way on the campaign trail every election cycle. Their programmes are the same - roads, hospitals, schools, water et al - so fundamentally; there is no difference between candidates A, B and C or party X, Y and Z. They are alter ego of themselves so it's easy for them to meander and wander from one party to another. That is why party supporters gravitate towards candidates who have money to spend or to buy them during primaries not ideas or policies canvassed. That is why to create a differentiation; politicians and their followers play unhelpful, divisive and combustible religious, regional, tribal and ethnic cards hoping that non-discerning Nigerians who they have deluded will use those frivolities as differentiators in deciding who to vote for.

19.	We already have the knowledge base to solve our problems. The World Bank, the IMF, African Development Bank and other multilateral organizations give advice on what we can do to help ourselves. The United Nations agencies like UNIDO, UNCTAD, UNESCO, WHO, FAO, UNICEF; the African Union; the D8; the ECOWAS commission and so many other agencies and commissions also proffer solutions and provide technical assistances. Think tanks; conferences of professional organizations like ITU etc. provide expert support. Our politicians, public and civil servants regularly attend numerous seminars, conferences, trainings etc. in Nigeria and overseas aimed at finding solutions to our problems or empowering them with the knowledge and skills required to detect problems and or tackle identified challenges. We also organize workshops at different arms and levels of government. We even commission consulting firms to carry out studies and come up with implementable recommendations. I would say that all we need is available; the missing link is a proper enforcement, implementation and monitoring framework. We don't need to do anything special rather we just have to ensure the harvesting and harnessing of those ideas for the conceptualization and continuous review and refinement of government goals and targets; policies and programmes aimed at a better life for the Nigerian people and the establishment of robust frameworks for effective enforcement and implementation. This can only be achieved when leaders are not pursuing their personal interests at the expense of the state.

20.	Nigeria has enough plans on paper that can transform her into a 21st century economic wonder if implemented. The problem we have is that the pursuit of personal gains and interest by public officers and politicians, in whom we have vested the powers to act on our behalf, has derailed the implementation of those plans.

21.   One of the most beautiful things to behold is intelligence married to integrity; brains working together and in partnership with honesty.

22.   We should not take the challenges before us lightly. We have a society with a broken moral fiber and value system. We have a society that worships material things. We have a society with millions of hectares of fertile lands but which spend billions of dollars importing food it can produce. We have a society where tens of millions of able-bodied citizens are unemployed. We have a society where utilities are not working efficiently. We have a society with decrepit infrastructure. However, "a ruling class that sees the state solely as a means of expropriating public resources is incapable of good governance. Such a class will, by its character abuse power" according to a foremost African scholar, Tunde Obadina. Should our hope for a serious approach and solution to the challenges before us then lie in the emergence of a new elite class?

23.   The erudite professor Itse Sagay was quoted to have said that Nigeria has a "rapacious, exploitative and buccaneering political elite class who are in government to pursue personal comfort and pleasure and not to serve the Nigerian people"? Do you concur?

24.   "To befoul the alliance between corrupt business and corrupt politics is the first task of the statesmanship of the day" – Theodore Roosevelt

25.	Our collective oath or resolve should be that we rather live in mud houses with straw roofs than steal public funds to build mansions.

26.	If we can build our houses very well by ensuring that we give it out to the right contractor at the right price; if we can build churches and mosques; why can't we regard government projects as the same? Why can't we contribute selflessly to the development of the private sector in this country by awarding contracts to competent and deserving firms and be content with what we have while deriving joy from the success of others in the profession they have chosen for themselves? Why should public and civil servants award government contracts sometimes to themselves and or to their incompetent and unqualified cronies at inflated rates for their own personal benefits? Why should members of the National Assembly be collecting contracts from ministries, departments and agencies they are supposed to oversight for themselves and or cronies? Is this how we are going to develop corporations that will create jobs in Nigeria? When the gate keepers and custodians of our values are guilty of violating them, what then is our hope?

27.	Nigeria seems to have one of the most vibrant and active political elite class in the world. The only snag is that a greater portion of their vivacity is transactional while some are sentimental and have no clear broad based conceptual and philosophical underpinning. These lead to a whole lot of noise about insignificant and irrelevant issues like power shift and power rotation which benefit individual politicians and their cliques not the society as some may want us to believe. It therefore seems as if Nigeria has the most unmindful, mentally lazy, morally weak and vicious, if not unwise elite class in the world hence transformation and reformation should start from them.

28.   Our politics need upgrading because it is not organized or structured to be proactive and pre-emptive. We are reactive, not responsive. For example, if our politics had a place for foresight, imagination and responsiveness, we would have known that we need a sound electoral system to build a democratic culture for development. On the contrary, it took us the shambolic elections of 1999, 2003 and 2007 plus the attendant chaos, loss of lives and property for us to know that our democracy is being endangered by electoral malpractices. We then acted right by amending the electoral law in 2010 for the 2011 elections though some of the provisions are still not being enforced. Again, it took us the crisis in the Niger Delta for us to know that the fiscal regimes in the oil and gas sector does not support oil producing communities and give them a sense of ownership in the sector before we came up with the petroleum industry bill (PIB). Incidentally the bill is yet to be passed into law. Why? Maybe we are waiting for another round of turmoil in the Niger Delta as we cannot anchor peace in that region on the perpetual pacification of former militants. Why must we always be forced to act by crisis? Why can't we foresee crisis and act to stop or prevent it from occurring? Why must we wait for Jos to go up in flames in 2001, 2008, and 2010 for us to attempt doing something serious to check the crisis even though we are yet to get to its root? Why is our politics so slow to respond to our

development challenges? Perhaps it's because there is too much personal and sectional pursuit. If we allow the interest of all Nigerians and not selfish or clannish interest to guide our actions, we will reach consensus in good time before things get worse or out of hand.

29.　　Leadership vision check: If you want to know if you truly love and have a vision for your country, look inwards. If your mind is filled with the goodies you will acquire while in office and not the opportunities you will create and spread to your people even at a personal expense; it means you don't have a vision for your country and will not be remembered for anything noble.

CHAPTER TWO

Leadership Excellence

30.　　The generation that will better Nigeria will be the generation whose political class will be preoccupied with finding solutions through debates as against quarrelling over patronage.

31.　　It is very important for our political leaders to know that their primary responsibility is to help their people obtain the basic necessities of life such as food, shelter and clothing which in modern times has become nutrition, accommodation and fashion. People have need not just to eat but to take nutritious meals with varieties; people have need not just for shelter but for comfortable accommodation; people have need not just for clothing but to be fashionable and look good with reasonable change of clothes. And basic to all these three is people's need for a stable source of income, freedom and security. The government should create an atmosphere and environment that gives all its citizens equal opportunity and level playing field to achieve all these. There should be no discrimination against anybody or giving someone undue advantage because of the color of his or her skin, tribe, religion or political leaning. This is necessary because an all-inclusive society demonstrates that the government is for us all, that the society belongs to us all and that we all have a stake in its wellbeing.

32.   An exceptional leader has a vision for a great and modern society. That vision cannot be achieved in an unethical environment where people think only for themselves and worship material things. It cannot be achieved in a society where people have no values and no regard for the law. Ethics, the right values, discipline, integrity, worthy principles and conviction is foundational and sine qua non to achieving it. A great leader with a great vision will always ask himself, what can I do to make my society ethical so that I can achieve this honorable vision of mine which is to contribute to building a modern society characterized by equity, fairness, justice, peace and economic progress etc.? Achieving a more ethical society will be one of his major priorities and this entails that he can't engage in unethical acts.

33.   A great leader has a vision for the good of all and therefore will not support or condone schemes or acts that will confer benefits on a select few at the expense of many. Therefore, a leader will ensure that due process is followed at all times.

34.   Addressing our challenges need a sense of urgency, focused attention and a transformational vision.

35.   The ideas a person has, his values and his passion, dedication and commitment to the notion of selfless sacrificial service are qualities that should distinguish him for leadership.

36.   We need a leadership cohort who judges their progress and success based on societal progress and development; that see themselves as progressing if the society at large is progressing. A cohort whose judgment of societal progress and development is objectively based on global development indicators, parameters and metrics not subjectively based on narrow and limited focus on road construction and other mundane things which are normal government duties and responsibilities christened dividends of democracy.

37.   We need to raise leaders – politicians, civil servants, public servants, professionals' et al – who will make a difference. We need to produce leaders who will advocate for and protect people's rights instead of leaders who will rather betray the people to achieve their own personal and selfish interests.

38.   "Progress in every age result only from the fact that there are some men and women who refuse to believe that what they knew to be right cannot be done"- Russel W. Davenport.

39.   You become a leader when you are able to put your beliefs into words and marshal it out in writing. Those who believe in what you believe in will file behind you to actualize it.

40.   We have to acknowledge what has been done without dwelling too much and too long on them. What has been done need not be done again and therefore are history or belong to the past. However, we should constantly look at areas that require improvements or upgrades and areas not yet covered; we should concentrate on things not done well and things yet to be done. That's the pursuit of excellence.

41.   It seems our political elite class thrives on promoting primitive tendencies of clamoring for power shift on the basis of religion, regions and other trivial issues among the citizenry rather than seeding the culture of demanding for excellence and good governance in them.

42.   You have a vision when your resolve cannot be overcome by pleasure and comfort or weakened by momentary hardship; conviction is vision.

43.   If the four tyres of a car are bad, and you repair only one, the car will not move. The one tyre you repaired will also not move. The driver's job is to coordinate efforts aimed at fixing all the tyres so that he can move. Likewise, you can't fix one part of Nigeria without the rest and expect the country to move forward. A national leader thinks for the nation like the driver of a car. Late Dr. Nnamdi Azikiwe of blessed memory is an example of a

National Leader. On the other hand, a regional leader thinks for her region. A state leader thinks for his state while a local leader thinks for his locality. It is therefore wrong for local, state or regional leaders to blackmail, stampede or attempt to railroad national leaders with national mindsets to become regional, state or local advocates simply because he comes from or hails from their constituency. Like the driver of a car, the national leader recognizes the fact that for the nation to move forward, the constituent parts - the tyres - have to be in proper shape. He therefore coordinates; supports and enables efforts aimed at ensuring that the component parts of the country are working very well. He cannot concentrate on one part to the detriment of another because he knows that if he does so, he will fail to achieve national progress which is his goal. Therefore, people have to lead based on their ken and abilities and we should be able to know where someone belongs. Local, state and regional leaders have their sphere of influence and roles in the society. They should recognize that national leaders also occupy a different sphere and stop attempting to conscript them into their own local spheres through blackmail. This nugget was informed by the write up of a popular newspaper columnist with a popular Nigerian newspaper who referred to (then) Vice President Namadi Sambo as a northern politician, "who refused to provide a rallying point for an agitated north". The columnist found himself on the wrong foot when I reached out to him and asked him "what ails the northern part of Nigeria that doesn't ail the south and why vice president Namadi Sambo should provide a rallying point for an agitated north instead of providing a rallying point for an agitated nation?"

44.   On what basis are citizens mobilized in politics in Nigeria today? Nigerians are mobilized along combustible fault lines of ethnicity, tribalism, geography and religion. We should seek ways to correct this anomaly because it is a serious issue that is threatening safety and security in the nation. Nigerian citizens are being wounded, maimed and murdered in cold blood on account of contestations for power and leadership positions on false grounds yet we sleep comfortably. This indeed is callous and demonstrates our utter disregard for the sanctity of human life despite our profuse expression of religious vivacity. How can normal and sane human beings who claim to be leaders and their followers, engage in activities with the potentials to cause unrest and the loss of lives under the pretext of canvassing for votes or contesting for public offices? A true leader values life because he knows that the fellow who might die or get killed, despite how remote and interior the area this occurs, maybe someone who would have nurtured another Aminu Kano, M.K.O Abiola, Emeka Anyaoku, Prof. Wole Soyinka, Prof. Chinua Achebe, Prof. Dora Akunyili, Kanu Nwankwo, Chimamanda Adichie, Asa, Pete Edochie, Justice Chukwudifu Oputa, Aliko Dangote or any of our favorite statesmen, sports men and women, professionals, musicians, artists, authors, businessmen et al who have won us global acclaim and brought us dignity and honor around the world.

These avoidable deaths, oblivious to us, might as well be that of our own Winston Churchill, Abraham Lincoln, Nelson Mandela, Henry Ford, J.P Morgan, Albert Einstein, John Lennon, Warren Buffet, Bill Gate, Mark Zuckerberg or other great leaders, scientists, entrepreneurs or inventors.

Nigerians who are dying needlessly and who are being killed – some by the system and security agencies – may be those who would have someday become stars and great achievers in various fields of human endeavor and tremendously contribute to our forward march. We should therefore wake up and stand up for the sanctity of life. We should say no to the divisive politics of region, religion and ethnicity which often lead to incitements and violence. We should say no to political killings. Every Nigerian has the right to life; the Nigerian people and state should be organized to guarantee that.

45.   As a country with very steep development challenges, our politics should reflect the urgency of our situation. We don't need business as usual, don't rock the boat, rub my back I rub your back politics. We don't need ordinary, average or so-so leadership. We need quality, top-notch, extraordinary and exemplary leadership. We need leaders who are ready to make sacrifices for the people. That is to say politicians should not earn obscene allowances when most agencies of government have no money for operations to carry out their mandate. Contract award should not be done by politicians but should be undertaken by a procurement board made up of seasoned and mature professional procurement experts at local, state and federal levels of government. Recruitment into government agencies must follow due process. The responsibility of the politician will be to ensure that law and order is maintained, projects executed, good implementable policies formulated and the citizenry mobilized for development. When these are done, there will be less political tension because the urge to go into politics will be less since there will be no money to be made as there will be no carcasses for scavengers. Since

where the carcasses are, the vultures gather; it therefore follows that where there are no carcasses, vultures will not gather. When people realize that you don't need to have someone in government house to achieve your goals, nobody will care where the occupant of that office comes from. This is very important because politics and elections in Nigeria has become a battle, a do or die affair, a war without rules of engagement; an ill wind that blows no one any good which has to stop.

I don't need to include articles of violence that have taken place in the country from 1999 till date on account of politics to make us come to terms with the fact that the situation is very grave and need urgent attention. This is because if care is not taken, political violence might take over from Boko Haram in the scale of destruction of life and property. Should we wait for that to happen before we attempt to remedy the situation? Politics must as a matter of urgency and as an imperative for sustainable development and peace, be made economically unattractive but socially rewarding.

46.   To reduce tension in the polity, we need to make the siting of projects a scientific issue that is not determined by the whims and caprices of individuals. This can be done by developing scientific models in all sectors and levels of government for locating and establishing projects. For instance, we can have a map of the road networks yet to be built. The scientific basis for deciding the roads to be done first should be the population that will benefit and its direct impact on the economy. Assuming an LG, a state and the Federal Government has two roads within their sphere they want to work on, one leading to an industrial layout and another to a populous

town, the first one to be done might according to the model any of the tiers of government is using be the one leading to the industrial layout because it will boost employment creation, income generation and tax receipts. The money generated from the tax produced by the industrial layout can now be used to build the road leading to the populated town afterwards. Same goes to health, schools and others. If this is done, we will have a more organized society as the fight or clamor for political office mainly for the purpose of outmaneuvering others to attract so called development projects to one's constituency will stop since locating government projects is technically governed with scientific models, not whimsically determined by politicians and public office holders and so-called power brokers.

47.   Infrastructures such as roads, schools, hospitals and the rest do not require any extraordinary genius to put in place. Firms that can produce world class designs and execute the projects are many in Nigeria and most of them are even looking for work to do. We should therefore leave our mediocre and elementary fixation with such things and move to a sophisticated horizon. We need to move to a more elevated vista where, on the demand side, the need of the people and the society are scientifically identified, quantified and prioritized. Subsequently, the projects and programmes to address those needs are scientifically determined, expertly designed and technically executed (based on already set priorities which decide the ones to be done first) with all the best practices of project management and contract delivery complied with. Examples of such best practices can be cost minimization by reducing material wastages

among others; adherence to quality standards and getting value for money. On the supply side, the government then looks at its revenue sources and put in place measures to increase it which will include plugging loopholes and leakages by ensuring transparency and accountability in revenue management. The government can also establish frameworks – legal, institutional and regulatory to ensure optimum exploitation of all its natural resources. This therefore means that the sustainable expansion of the revenue base should also be seen as one of the so-called dividends of democracy. Judging competence and achievement or performance in office using the local parlance should span the entire gamut. From the foregoing, no serious government in a majority world country will have the time to make too much noise and organize events and parties around the inauguration of roads, junction improvements, street lights, immunization programmes, hospitals and the rest because its hand will be full. The government will be focused on governance and save money used for adverts and publicity in the mass media by making the information about its achievement available in less expensive and easily accessible format for citizens, researchers, investors and other interested parties. It will engage in social mobilization and sensitization activities where necessary and wait for election time to make its scorecard known to the electorates.

48.   "By now, politicians should be telling us how they want to change our 200 years old-hoe technology into modern forms from local inputs. In the architectural world, politics ought to, by now, be popularizing mud as a main source in building technology, instead of cement because

those houses built (with mud) over 200 years ago are still standing and enduring." – A former Dean of the Faculty of Social Sciences, University of Nigeria, Nsukka, Prof. Okwudibia Nnoli, deploring the poverty of ideas prevalent among the political class and asking public office holders, especially politicians, to set the agenda for Nigeria's transformation.

49.   We need to assess where we are and the kind of leadership that brought us here. We need to put our challenges in perspective proportionally and juxtapose it with the kind of leadership that will solve them. We also need to determine where we want to go and the kind of leadership that will take us there. In any case, 'agbata ekee' (an Igbo language term for people working in group and sharing the proceeds among themselves after work for the day, often derogatory and reserved for touts) leaders won't take us anywhere. We need leaders who see material things as toys and derive pleasure and satisfaction from social progress and advancement rather than the acquisition of assets with resources whose sources they can't defend.

50.   We have levels of leadership in the society or community. We know that leaders play a very important role in mobilizing, informing, enlightening and educating the people. We also know that the leaders' psychology, philosophy and worldview affect the led. Have we taken out time to review the leadership levels we have in our communities; how they are selected, their qualifications, the peoples' expectation from them, their daily tasks and duties and how those tasks and duties are performed, their understanding of their roles and its place in

reinforcing their good nature and getting the people properly focused? Is there any programme aimed at teaching them the concept of sacrifice in leadership so that they don't see their position as an opportunity to feather their nest to the detriment of their people? Is there any programme in place to train them (leaders) continually to meet their communities' expectation and our standard as a nation? As a nation, we have to develop what we expect from the traditional institution and give them all the tools they need to meet it.

51.   It is dishonest for any elected political cohort to say they can't overhaul a society within four years - some so still fail after eight years. It is absolutely possible though development is more of incremental than sudden. The way to go is to ensure that the society is on the right path or track: To reform and strengthen agencies of government responsible for planning – planning cities and maintaining the plan; reform and strengthen agencies of government responsible for the enforcement of law, order and justice, equity and fair play; strengthen structures and mechanisms for gathering information for decision making; initiate policies that will better the lives of citizens and enable them attain their full potentials; ensure that equality before the law is real and allow the law and policies to order and focus the society. Development doesn't necessarily need to be instant but the most important thing is that the society should be moving in the direction of gradual, incremental positive or progressive change. This does not need ages to achieve; it's about having the right conceptual framework and can be accomplished in less than four years, not to talk of eight years.

52.	Most of the things our present crop of political leaders are celebrating as achievements are things that should have been done 50, 40, 30 or 20 years ago; power supply, highways and water supply for instance. We should divide our development deficits into what should have been done in the past that has not been done which we shouldn't make too much noise about when they are eventually done; and what should be done today to make our society modern and 21st century compliant like high speed rail and broad band internet infrastructure among others. These are things we should celebrate. The former just amount to making up which does not deserve rolling out the drums.

53.	Why should a Nigerian political party be founded on building roads, providing portable water and other basic needs? Political parties should rather be founded on principles behind these projects such as the percentage of the materials and manpower content that should be local and how it can be enforced or achieved. The main push of political parties should be on the priority's government should give to important issues and the means of achieving them. Their focus should be on how the government should generate money and utilize it efficiently. They should be preoccupied with identifying areas of waste in government and how they can be plugged instead of creating or being conduits for waste.

54.	"One of the true tests of leadership is the ability to recognize a problem before it becomes an emergency"- Arnold Glasow, American Humorist.

55.   "Intellectuals solve problems, geniuses prevent them"- Albert Einstein.

56.   Nigerian elites should study what it takes to build a nation and commit to it for the rapid transformation of the country.

CHAPTER THREE

Institutional Integrity

57.   Most of our institutions are not functioning properly and it seems as if they are deliberately weakened by being designed with loopholes. The ambiguities then give some people in strategic gatekeeping positions the leeway and leverage to abuse their offices and positions. Some corner for themselves revenues that should have gone into the coffers of these organizations to enable them function well and to develop organically. Also, on the expenses side, they spend more than they should to procure goods and services. The excesses are allegedly creamed off and go into the private pockets and bank accounts of approving officers, paying officers and conniving businessmen and women. The institutions are sucked and plundered from the money inflow (revenue) avenue and the money outflow (expenses) avenue to the benefit of a tiny few and the detriment of those who work in those institutions in particular and millions of Nigerians in general. This therefore creates a few wealthy citizens whose wealth have no story - of ingenuity, hard work, entrepreneurship, production, invention, or innovation in product or service delivery that creates wealth and add value to the economy — behind it. They own big palatial mansions, shopping malls, housing estates, hotels and even private jets etc. in Nigeria and overseas. At the other end of the spectrum are poorly motivated staffs and a large mass of pauperized citizens who find themselves in a hopeless and desperate situation. With the state of affairs presently, it is obvious that this deliberate weakening of public establishments to satisfy the greed of a few is not helping us. We therefore need to re-organize our systems,

define functions and roles properly to plug these loopholes if our institutions must serve the interest of the majority.

58.   Assuming we have 500 government ministries, agencies and parastatals with project exchange points in terms of contract awards and payment for executed contracts; the public officers who are key decision makers in each exchange point that form the cabal of contract awards and payment for kickbacks and other personal favors and gains are like 20 individuals. 20x500 is 10,000. What this means is that 10,000 (0.00005%) Nigerians are the key persons nurturing corruption in a country of about 200,000,000 people thereby stunting growth and holding the country down. Conversely, they hold the key to its greatness. If all of these 10,000 public servants put their feet down and decide that they will follow due process and procedures in contracts award and payment of contractors without collecting bribes or kickbacks for at least 10years, you will not recognize Nigeria in another 10 years. We will achieve, in the succeeding 10 years of rectitude and discipline, 10 times what we achieved the preceding 10 years of impunity and indiscipline.

59.   One of the things we failed to do in the early days of this republic was to conduct a study on the extent to which the military has distorted or defaced our institutions - like the police, the judiciary, the legislature, the executive arm of government, the civil service, the business environment, and even the academia – against a model of what they should be in a democracy and start working towards their restoration. It is still not too late for us to do that because the carbuncles of military dictatorship are

still with us – in our institutions and systems – and constitutes a drag on our progress.

60.   There should be transparency, openness and accountability in the management of government business.

61.   If corruption stops in Nigeria today, it doesn't mean that we'll have an el-dorado. No, it means that we have placed our country on a platform where we can progressively develop it through hard work. At present, where corruption is still endemic: the result we are getting is slow progress.

62.   Procurement and contracting have been going on in this country for years. Does it mean that the awarding agencies have not been able to recognize reputable companies with good performance track records to keep executing contracts while patronizing new entrants who show good promise based on their technical and financial appeal once in a while? For goodness sake, why should we have the highest number of abandoned projects in the world?

63.   Though individuals are generally good, they are not dependable. This is not to say that they are bad, it's just that they have limitations and weaknesses and can fail you when you least expect it or when you need them most. We all at one point or another, knowingly or unknowingly have disappointed people who had certain expectations from us. As it is said, the spirit might be willing but the ability is not there. That is why the progress of any society cannot be built around the virtues and magnanimity of

individuals. What should be dependable are systems underpinned by institutions. Therefore, the greatest achievement that should be attributed to a politician should be how he has been able to refine and advance the system to make it more efficient and responsive to peoples' need. Citizens' preoccupation will then be to understand how the system works so that they can leverage on it to achieve their goals of financial independence which of course will rub off positively on the economy rather than waste precious time in endless praise-singing, bootlicking, genuflection and running rings around politicians for favors and peanuts.

64.   Should the business community be blamed for official corruption and abuse of public office by politicians and civil servants? I don't think they are culpable. They only follow the officially or unofficially established ground rules they meet in the system. The heartbeat of a modern society (a great economy, stable and just society) is a system that encourages, promotes and enables citizens to pursue their political, social and economic goals decently and legally. A system that allows them to freely go about their economic activities without compelling them to engage in unethical and corrupt practices to achieve set objectives. That is the structure and framework upon which any society can be developed and it's one of the primary reasons why the government and its institutions exist. A government should work to guarantee that.

65.   If the (rural) people themselves cannot wake up and use their ballot well by voting according to their conscience and standing behind their vote, then there is no hope for change in their circumstances. Do we then

leave them to their fate? Mass education and enlightenment is the panacea. Whose responsibility is it to educate and enlighten voters or citizens? It is the duty of the media, NGOs, Political Parties, INEC; Community Development Associations (CDOs), Religious Organizations, Opinion leaders', Government agencies like NOA to educate the people. All stakeholders should therefore wake up to this essential responsibility.

66.   The politics of the country has been so muddled up and polarized along ethnic, regional and religious lines that young Nigerians have become disillusioned to the point of hopelessness. This has driven many to consider what is wrong like bribing to get contracts or jobs as normal. This orientation needs to be reversed by issue-based politics and diligent law enforcement which makes bad examples of the lawless to discourage youths from normalizing wrong doing.

67.   Vanguard, Tuesday, April 30, 2013 pg. 49. Reported that 'The Quantity Surveyors Registration Board of Nigeria (QSRBN) blamed the current high cost of construction projects on the exclusion of quantity surveyors from performing their cost functions… President of QSRBN, Mallam Hussaini Adamu Dikko, who stated this at the maiden stakeholders' conference in Abuja called for patriotic action to block money leakages in the construction industry which according to him, had put construction costs in Nigeria highest above what is obtainable anywhere in the world'.

68.   The series of riots and violence that has taken place in this country either sparked by religion or otherwise

should be seen purely as a social and security issue. It is a failure of law enforcement for these crimes to take place without anybody being caught and successfully prosecuted for extra-judicial murder (this security challenge has been exacerbated by the culture of sentiment). We need to strengthen our law enforcement agencies and apparatus and allow the law, aptly described as an ass, to work no matter whose ox is gored.

69.   Businessmen and politicians should be treated with suspicion and considered by bureaucrats as 'rats' from whom they, like 'cats', are to protect the 'valuables' of the state. However, when bureaucrats connive with businessmen and politicians to swindle a state, then that state would really be despoiled and plundered. It's like the cat in the house meant to scare or catch rats turning into a rat and then inviting rats outside the house to come to party. Your guess is as good as mine. The challenge we have is that people who are supposed to be cats have turned into rats. This must change for Nigeria to rise.

70.   Our justice system should be remedial and correctional rather than oppressive and punitive. For the past fourteen years, our political leaders have not reformed the police and judiciary (which were left comatose during the military era) enough to meet up with the demands and norms of democratic governance and existence. It's still not too late for them to do so.

71.   If our system is not organized, why then do people go to work? I think the purpose of work is to keep a system working in a structured manner. Therefore, if the system is disorganized, we should investigate if people are

really working for the achievement of organizational objectives and or probe the structure of work – most especially our civil service; whether it is properly organized, aligned and integrated to achieve objectives.

72.   The objectives of procurement laws are to ensure that contracts are given to qualified and competent contractors or companies that will execute them according to specifications at the right price with the interest of the nation coming first or paramount. The principle is that public officers should not use their office to advance personal interests.

73.   I hear a lot of people say they want to own this, they want to own that; they want to get this, they want to get that; they want to become this, they want to become that. The issue is how? You realize that in an environment like ours, a lot of people are definitely going to achieve these goals by dishonest means either because they want to get it done that way or because it is difficult or seemingly tough to do it honestly. Our institutions and systems should make it easy for people to achieve their goals in good conscience.

74.   Corrupt public servants see themselves as 'businesspeople', the government institutions where they are supposed to be workers as 'a market', their offices as their 'shops' and the services they are supposed to provide to the public on behalf of the government for which they earn salaries and pensions as their 'wares'. Since the objective of traders is to make profit, the 'wares' are auctioned to the highest bidder and the proceeds go into

their private pockets. We need to find a way to stop the misdemeanors.

75.   It's unlawful for civil servants to collect bribes and gratifications from businessmen for contracts and other favors. Also, it is criminal for businessmen to induce civil servants with bribes. Still, despite the fact that it's illegal, some businesspeople thrive on cutting deals with civil servants and offering them bribes as sweeteners to get what they want. After careful analysis, I realized that some businesses will give bribes for contracts for three reasons; 1. They don't have corporate values and philosophy and most of the time they are conduits for public servants 2. Some businesses depend on the government for revenues. The government constitutes 90% or 100% of their market therefore without government patronage, they will die. As a result, they will do whatever it takes to get government contracts; by hook or by crook. 3. Real businesses that have a desire for profit maximization and to meet targets. If they mix it with greed and ignore their corporate social responsibility, corporate values and philosophy, they will give bribes to win contracts so as to meet those targets. Generally, without excusing businessmen for engaging in bribery and corruption, civil servants are the real culprit for all official bribery and corruption not businessmen. This is because the businessman has more pressures than the civil servant. The businessman has competitors who want to get the same job or contract, therefore if he realize that giving bribe will make him win the contract over competitors, he will do it if he is desperate to get the contract. He also feels that if he doesn't deal, others will and he will consequently lose out. Almost all of the time he is desperate since he has to pay bills or make expenses

such as: office rent and maintenance; his salaries and staff salaries; employers portion of staff pension, compensation scheme, leave allowance; health and other insurances; transport, travels and accommodation; research and development; training; loan principal and interest payments; levies and permits; internet and communications; utilities; security; purchase of business assets such as machinery and equipment; assets maintenance, income tax, education tax and many more. He has his family and dependents to worry about. In fact, he is like a mini-government. He needs to get contracts to pay these bills hanging over his neck since Nigeria has no bankruptcy protection for businessmen who fail. He doesn't have access to single digit loan to restructure his business if he experiences cash flow crunch. Most public servants take advantage of these to lure businessmen into corrupt practices or succumb to the pressures from unethical, burdened and desperate businessmen who offer them bribes. Since both can offer and receive bribes without sanctions and coupled with the fact that easy money is addictive, they keep doing it. My outlook is that civil servants hold the key to ending official bribery and corruption or cash (and other favors) for contract schemes in Nigeria. Though the civil servant is not well paid comparatively, he is less insecure. He is paid every month and gets his allowances regularly. He is entitled to pensions and gratuity. He has job security as he is rarely sacked. There is no need for him to compete with businessmen because both have chosen two different career paths. If he wants to do business, he should not use his office to confer advantage on himself. It is not allowed by civil service rules. He should live within his means, be content and do his job of protecting the integrity of the

Nigerian state. If civil servants insist on due process and adherence to rules and regulations, if they turn down advances and bribes, there is nothing businessmen or politicians can do about it. The public servant just has to refer them to the laws that empower him to do what he is doing which he has to do for the nation's greatness.

76.   Nigerians generally are peaceful people. The reason violence erupts in certain places is because in the first place, the mechanism for identifying flash points and nipping them in the bud is moribund. Secondly, the operational capacity of security agencies to intervene speedily in remote parts of the country to restore order when crisis erupts is weak.

77.   Nigeria seems to be a country where aggressive people who are ready to compromise make it. If you want to maintain your integrity, if you are honest, decent and cool, calm and collected; you seem not to stand a good chance. We have to work to change this scenario!

78.   Public servants should be able to derive pleasure and satisfaction from their accomplishments. They should be able to point to the achievements of their various offices in terms of the policies they have come up with and how it is reshaping the nation; in terms of the infrastructural projects they have conceived, initiated and completed and the difference it is making in people's lives (that is, how the people are benefiting from them) rather than the present craze for material wealth. I came across a public servant sometime in 2010 who works with the Federal Capital Development Authority in Abuja. He was narrating his contribution as a member of the committee

that oversaw the Gwarinpa Estate project with a glow in his eyes and so much joy. He noted that he doesn't own a house in Gwarinpa despite the fact that he has been on the board that oversaw its development. He recounted some of his other achievements in Abuja as it relates to parks etc. The encounter encouraged me and strengthened my faith in a brighter future for the country. All hope is not lost in this country after all, I muttered to myself. Against what some people will have us believe, we still have some decent, civilized, refined, ethical and incorruptible public servants in Nigeria.

79.   The relationship between politics and business has to be streamlined and made sacrosanct. The procurement process and other interfaces between the government and business and the project cycle should be made an area where a high degree of professionalism, integrity, rectitude, dedication, patriotism and other noble virtues are required. We urgently need to de-corrupt the project contracting, execution, monitoring and payment process.

80.   The seeming complexity of public finance nay budgeting in Nigeria is very troubling. Is budgeting no longer an estimate of income and expenditure? Is passing the budget not giving the executive the legal right to spend funds generated by the government on projects agreed on? When the government can't implement the budget, don't we have the right to know why? How much they got and how much they spent? Why are budgets not implemented? Why does it take years to pay contractors for jobs budgeted for by government and duly executed for government by them even when they have 'settled those to be settled'?

CHAPTER FOUR
Quality Citizenship

81.   The times should make us patriotically and sacrificially involved in politics.

82.   A common cliché in Nigeria is that the nation needs a miracle. If indeed Nigeria needs a miracle, it is a miracle within the capacity of every Nigerian citizen to perform. It is the miracle of at least abiding by the basic teachings of our religions whose places of worship we throng to every week. It is the miracle of doing the right thing and following due processes and procedures as enshrined in our laws, rules and regulations. It is the miracle of living up to the provisions of section 23 of the 1999 constitution as amended which states that "the national ethics shall be Discipline, Integrity, Dignity of Labor, Social Justice, Religious Tolerance, Self-Reliance and Patriotism." It is the miracle of at least answering the clarion call of our national anthem and honoring our national pledge. It is squarely in our hands to create the present and the future we desire for our nation instead of shifting to God, our simple and basic civic duties and responsibilities that doesn't require any extra-ordinary skill or talent to perform.

83.   Politicians by their very nature have a tendency to be selfish. In fact, Joseph Schumpeter likened them in a 1944 piece to bad horsemen who are more interested in remaining on a horse than the direction the horse is going. Politicians only respond to popular demand while statesmen respond to the need of the people. In our polity where statesmen are in short supply, looking up to our

politicians for so called transformation without active citizen participation or pressure is a pipe dream or illusion to say the least. We must get involved. If we want the police reformed, we must organize for it. If we want the government to fight corruption, we must demand for it; demonstrate that it is important to us, task the government on steps we should outline it must take to achieve that and punish failure at the polls without sentiments. Until we get involved, our society will remain underdeveloped. It is high time we stand up for what we want and deserve rather than sit down and waste precious time pontificating in vain.

84.   The greatest help which Nigeria need at the moment is the help of her citizens or put differently, the help of conscientious citizens in and outside government. Government technically speaking is a failure in this country. It seems the clique in power is deeply self-interested and not beholden to an ennobling ideology or fundamental objectives beyond self-preservation. On a personal level, some Nigerians through some dint of hard work and honesty have experienced tremendous transformation in the quality of their lives. Some have finished school, gotten jobs or established viable businesses and have settled down. Some have sojourned outside the country and are contributing positively to the economy of their host country through honest work. The hope of Nigeria firmly lies in the hands of these Nigerians who have achieved great success. They have to help by making tangible political contributions that will expand the frontiers of prosperity, peace and security for all. Besides, political contribution is one palpable way of ensuring that they touch every Nigerian positively and profoundly. Value

based political involvement is one way of ensuring that your talents, endowments and gifts rubs off or reflect on the nation. These honest Nigerians who have achieved good success should throw their hat into the political ring competitively or actively because they are Nigeria's hope.

85.   It is often said that one of the obligations of citizenship in a free society is eternal vigilance and observing what is happening around one; be it economic, social or political. Your alertness is to identify deviations from the norm and take steps with other free citizens through democratic and constitutional instruments or means to correct or nip them in the bud. This will ensure that they don't snowball into conflagrations that will hurt, consume or swallow the vulnerable, weak, uninsured, unprotected and exposed members of the society.

86.   If you give up on Nigeria, the country goes on for good and most probably for bad without you. Your involvement is just to be part of the process that ensures it goes on for good which should be your source of assurance, hope and optimism for a better Nigeria. This is because if you are not involved, there is no way of being sure that the right thing is being done or will be done. You cannot guarantee the success of a venture you are not part of. Therefore, get involved to guarantee a better Nigeria.

87.   We develop plans to build churches and mosques (places we have a heart attachment to), mobilize resources (people contribute based on their ability) and get the work satisfactorily done. What is the difference between building our places of worship to the highest

standard and quality specification based on the resources available to us and nation building? Nation building is also service to God and humanity. Our places of worship are usually our source of pride; our nation is also a source of pride. The difference between the two is that we normally don't quarrel about the details of building our places of worship but usually don't readily agree on the details of nation building though we agree we should build it. The divergence of opinions and sharp disagreements that arises from the modalities for nation building often makes a lot of us disillusioned and relegate our civic obligations to the background. We take solace in our religion and shut ourselves out from active participation and contribution to nation building that does not go beyond calls to pray for the nation. This ought not to be so. Under no pretext should we abdicate our civic responsibilities.

88.   Nigeria need mission driven political participation from its politicians and citizens not ambition and hunger driven political participation.

89.   Almost every Nigerian have political views or perspectives which they inflexibly cling to as right – the literate and illiterate; the educated and uneducated; those with high IQ and those with low IQ; those who have taken time to study the society and those who haven't; those who are knowledgeable and those who are not; people who have done business with government as contractors and consultants who know how our politicians and our wheeling and dealing bureaucracy works and those who have not stepped into any government ministry; those who have an idea or understanding of how things should be and those who have no understanding of the ideal;

those who read widely and those who have a phobia or aversion for reading; those who care about expert opinion or advise and those who have no regard for it; those who agree that problems are solved through research and scientific knowledge and those who don't know what research and scientific knowledge is all about - they think problems are solved by awarding contracts; those who see good governance as all-encompassing and those who see good governance as contract awards and construction projects not minding if the contract are properly designed, inflated or given to the wrong firm . They cling to their positions without regard to dialecticism (realizing the world is in a flux and the future likely to change) and intellectual humility (recognizing the limit of one's own knowledge) which are key aspects of wise reasoning or wisdom. They firmly hold onto their views with the swagger and assuredness of the spokespersons of deities or oracles and have no interest in subjecting their assessments to the rigors of intellectual analysis through debates. For them, whatever they wake up and conceive as right about politics, governance and the society is right; all other alternative views are rubbish.

Still, the issue remains; on what philosophy are our political views and perspectives built? What shapes it? What colors it? What illuminates it? What informs our views? Unfortunately, in most cases, those views are not informed by any sound philosophy, principle, ideology or scientific knowledge but by emotions, sentiments, petty grievances and outright ignorance. We need to use our common sense and common humanity to reason issues in politics and the society rather than pander to emotions or ethnic, religious and regional sentiments and miss the way.

90.   Basically, there has not really been any thorough work on the readiness of our politics to meet the challenges of our people. Our politics need re-phrasing; rephrasing of the debate, rephrasing of the issues; rephrasing of the purpose. Our politics need the right kind of citizens participation rooted in values and integrity. Our politics need to be better than what is obtained in more developed climes because the challenges we are facing here are greater than theirs.

91.   Who are you listening to? When you listen to people who speak high fustian languages and engage in rhetoric when addressing national issues without touching on the basic problems of Nigeria which are elite greed, official bribery, stealing and corruption that in turn bring out the worst in ordinary citizens, it is a pointer to something. It is a pointer to the fact that they are perpetrators and beneficiaries' unethical acts and corrupt practices. They have friends in local, states and federal governments who are politicians and public servants that they partner with to fleece the state and get what they think is their own share of the national cake. They are part of the numerous elite gangs that use the instrument of officialdom to enrich themselves and advance their personal interests at the expense of more than 100 million poor and impoverished Nigerians who are living on the margins of existence. They speak sparsely about corruption, turn it into semantics and often downplay its debilitating effect on the Nigerian polity by referring to political and social structures and institutions as the problem and that a national conference will solve it. Without emphasizing the need for effective law enforcement which of course will shut down their corrupt

sources; they speak as if there is a national conference whose result can be conclusive. They sell craps of faulty constitution to Nigerians as if there is anywhere in our present constitution that ask citizens to steal, collect bribes and engage in other forms of corrupt acts and practices.

They use the structure of Nigeria as an alibi for underdevelopment and prescribe convening a national conference as a solution knowing that the outcome of any constitutional conference will always be disputed. When they go to these conferences and come out with disagreements, they will continue in their unethical acts of self-enrichment using the instrument of government meanwhile pointing to unresolved constitutional issues as the reason why Nigeria is not developing. They will never point to impunity and lawlessness; absence of transparency and accountability in governance; lack of values and ethics in the conduct of government affairs which they are part of or guilty of as the reason for our underdevelopment. Therefore, 'knowing who you are listening' to is a wise admonition. Who is he? How did he make his money or how is he making his money? If he is someone who depends on government contracts to survive as a businessman or consultant, there is a 90% chance that he is compromised so don't take his grammar seriously because he has nothing to offer.

92.   We should avoid narrow mindedness, shallow thinking and lack of deep intellectual enquiry because they lead us to make irrational and unethical though seemingly logical demands. The Nigerian political space is filled with the din of power shift. The academia encouraged it by stridently demanding for the indigenization of vice

chancellorship years ago. Hitherto, the vice chancellor of a university can come from any part of the country, but that is no more because the vice chancellor of a university must come from the state where the university is located. Why do people clamor for power shift or power rotation most especially in Nigeria? It is because power is not being used to serve the right purpose. Power, unfortunately, is being wrongly exercised to favor one group or interest over the other rather than to accommodate the aspirations of all groups and interests in a fair, just, equitable and ethical manner. People therefore want power to come to them so that they can exercise it not differently but the way it has been abused by the fellow from the other divide. They are fed up with holding the wrong end of the stick so let the other divide suffer the injustice or the pains of not being in power. Is this supposed to be the way forward? Not at all. The demand for power shift instead of justice, fairness, rule of law, equity, ethics, due process, discipline et al is a product of mental laziness; the kind of lazy thinking that has made Africa a continent of war, underdevelopment and hunger.

93.   Most of our actions don't profoundly take the future into consideration in such a manner as to have a lasting influence on it. We have a patent lack of concern for the future. We are too obsessed about our present need that we erode our capacity to think rationally, engage in activities that might not be favorable to us as individuals in the meantime but which are capable of creating a better future for ourselves and our children. Like beasts, we allow nature and fate to decide what our future will be and use religious platitudes to cover or gloss over this abdication of responsibility. It is important for us

to understand that what we do is not only about today but tomorrow and the future. You should not, because you are hungry, eat all your seeds. The fact that you have tomorrow on your radar means that you will creatively look for how to satisfy your hunger and reserve your seeds knowing that if you eat them, you are inviting lack, destitution and probably death the next year. We should understand that what we do in our offices as civil servants, public servants and private sector people is not about today but tomorrow. If we do business or engage in actions without adequate thought about the future impact of those actions, we are being animalistic. It is only animals that don't have the future implication of their actions to worry about - nature decides the course of their existence.

94.   Intellectual dishonesty is one of our retarding or retrogressive forces.

95.   Politics like engineering, medicine, surveying and other profession has become a career in this country since the military left the scene in 1999. Like other noble professions, have we made any attempt to define the philosophy that should underpin politics in this country? What I'm saying is; upon which philosophy is politics built in this country? Is it built on the philosophy of selfless service to humanity and social justice or is it built on the philosophy of election violence and rigging, stealing, lying, plunder, power shift and rotation, mediocrity, ethnicity, gangsterism, lawlessness, materialism, greed, sybaritism and other negative vices one can think of? We should be able to sincerely answer this question or else all these attempts at constitutional change, single tenure suggestions among others as the way forward are mere

delusions. I think it's high time we begin to refocus our debates and questions. We should ask our politicians what they have done to create a fairer, competitive, equitable and just society which is very vital for peace and security in a community rather than all these focus on roads, health centers, and other poorly planned, badly executed and highly inflated infrastructure projects. What do we really care about as a society? What are we really living for as a people? What are we passionate about? What is our essence?

96.   In a society where politicians climb rostrums to narrate how they are constructing or have constructed schools, hospitals, street lights, guest houses and the likes – with almost 80% imported materials and inputs like doors etc. – as if they are construction site managers and are venerated and praised for infrastructure projects when their job description actually goes beyond that; it takes a very good observer and thinker to realize that such past times or practices are outdated, to question the propriety and adequacy of such one sided performance measurement and evaluation parameters which lack balance, robustness and sincerity.

97.   Nigerians seem to respond to leadership but unfortunately can't influence leadership. It means that they are at the mercy of their leaders. If they have good leaders, well for them because they will follow. If they have bad rulers, bad for them because they can't resist misrule for their own good. It's not in them perhaps because they got independence on a platter of gold or because of ethnic, regional, religious and class sentiments.

98.   For Nigeria to develop politically, citizens not only the civil society must develop the capability to engage the government. The people that should set the pace anyway are the elites. When the elites are interested in (or are bought over with) government contracts, appointments and patronage, who will rebuke the government when it strays? That's part of the crisis in our political development; lack of genuine citizen participation and engagement with the government championed by the elite class. The opposition is not suited to do this at the moment because when they get into government, they still do the same things.

99.   We need to overcome disillusionment, cynicism and apathy so as to work to make our country great.

100.   We seem to lack the awareness, social consciousness, grit and organizational capacity to come together in a group or as a community to do what is right for our neighborhood and society or to collectively close ranks against injustice and exploitation in a focused, objective, principled and sustainable manner.

101.   The missing link in Nigeria's democracy and development is citizens' rational, objective, intelligent and value-based participation in politics. Poverty, prejudices, sentiments and emotions fueled by religion, ethnicity, regionalism and clannishness blur it.

102.   Our society is unwilling to objectively quantify the contribution of public office holders to social progress. They are rather judged based on how well they have done for themselves in office. For example, if someone wins an

election, the society adjudges the person to be lucky; to have made it; that he will never be poor again. This is because the dominant mindset is that he has secured a ticket to wealth and riches. The public office holder's duties and responsibilities are mooted. After office, he or she is not held to high standard of evaluation to establish how s/he suddenly became stupendously rich. There is no means of ascertaining how s/he made his or her money within a space of few years. Life goes on. Yet the people expect development. What an illusion?

103.   We should not underestimate the capacity of folks to engage in intelligent discourse and debate based on common sense if that is put forward as the way they can better their lives and change their circumstances.

104.   The truth is that people still contribute financially to the development of their communities. If indigenes can dip their hands into their pockets to contribute to community development, why can't they organize themselves within that same framework to demand accountability from elected officials? The reasons are;

- The institutional arrangements in the country do not support that. The security and law enforcement agencies are neither structured nor empowered to fight nor support those who fight political criminals. As a result, the people can't do it for fear of recrimination.
- Nigerians desire for infrastructural development is so overwhelming that they are willing to do anything including praising an elected official to high heavens, indulging his every whim and excesses and perhaps even send him gifts so

that he will look upon their community favorably. Under this scenario, no community leader or association will like to engage in such acts as questioning an elected or selected political office holder. Opposition is viewed with dismay in communities and seen as anti-development by many.

•	It takes a radical and independent individual (who are few and in very short supply in Nigeria) to break ranks and question the abuse of authority or power and champion the cause of prudence, transparency and accountability. Even at that, it is customary for leaders of his community to pay a visit to the governor or public officer involved to pledge their loyalty to him and disown their son even if he is saying the truth.

They will tell him not to mind the radical, that he is an irritant, that his views about the governor or local government chairman are his personal views and not that of the community leadership. That as far as they are concerned, the governor or local government chairman is a great man and an uncommon transformer.

It is only chronic, debilitating and persistent neglect and marginalization that can force a community to close ranks and challenge the abuse of office.

105.	The fact of the matter still remains that in Nigeria presently, there are things that has to be done that are not being done and things that are being done that are not supposed to be done. The issue now is; what are those things?

106.   Political change requires commitment and hard work; it is not a tea party.

CHAPTER FIVE

Embrace Positive Values

107. Individuals are born into a society — with a government in place — when they come into the world and this is without their consent since they didn't have to choose the society or nation whose citizen they would like to be. Growing up — despite the society they find themselves — their dreams like everyone else is to be comfortable materially in terms of the three basic needs of man namely food, shelter and clothing; to have their homes and families; to be free; to be secure and to be healthy among others. To achieve these, they follow a template that has long been established by the society and refined by reformers before they were born. Led or guided by their parents or guardians, they start with going to schools, becoming members of religious groups and other social organisations. As they grow, they bond with their families and begin to make friends. In the midst of all these coming of age activities, they begin to find out that there are challenges. Making it through school is quite a grind. Graduating from school is a lot of work but they give it their best shot and revel in their successes. Getting the dream job after graduation is not easy either. Settling into the job is a different kettle of fish with office politics and pressures to contend with. Conversely, they may find out that learning skills, vocations or trades is tough. One has to be at his best to win and retain customers and clients so as to make a living. They brave the odds nonetheless. Going forward, they realize that most of the problems they have to battle with in life (like not receiving their $500 monthly allowances for seven months from a government that gave them scholarship to study in foreign countries - with

student visas - where the cost of living averages $750 per month) are unnecessary. They find out that these troubles are as a result of man-made political, social and economic factors within and beyond their control. The factors beyond their control are dealt with through faith (religion). The real challenge is to identify the factors within their control. This is necessary so that they don't push what they are supposed to do to God which can be ruinous because God won't do our jobs for us but can only help us do them. Proper identification of what are in their powers to deal with will enable them to take the right steps or agree with others on the right course of action to be taken to eliminate or mitigate them. Take politics for instance, they might realize that there are things that are not working well in government which are affecting the society negatively. They realize that there are certain practices instituted and sustained in the system like official bribery, stealing and corruption that are not right. These strictures need to be reformed for the society to move forward for the good of all its inhabitants. However, the system is resilient and in the course of attempting to achieve their material goals they might still have to deal with the system as it is — pre or before the change they envision kicks in — depending on the career they have chosen or their position in their chosen field. Dealing with the system as it is means that they will compromise and lose the moral authority to successfully bring about or initiate positive changes. This is where the real choice which will determine the course of their lives comes in. They have to make a choice (1) to be agents of change (2) to be neutral and not be involved in activism for change and (3) to be part of the impunity and indiscipline. The decision made at this stage produces four kinds of citizens.

i.   Citizens who will not like to do business with the corrupt system and will love to be part of efforts to reform and change it.

ii.   Citizens who will not like to do business with the corrupt system because they don't want to soil their hands or scar their consciences but will not want to be part of reform and change efforts due to fear and ignorance.

iii.   Citizens who will like to do business with the corrupt system because they are morally weak or as a result of certain exigencies or pressures - as if they are the only ones with exigencies - but agree that it has to be reformed and changed but don't want to be involved.

iv.   Citizens who like to do business with the corrupt system and do not agree that change is needed because the status quo favors them. They don't want their undue advantages to end. Citizens in category (i) who genuinely want to be part of social rebirth so that their generation can bequeath a better society to the next – for that is how civilization flows – will have to seek to make a living in careers and trades that will not compromise them.

Those who don't care about change deal with the system as it is. Some will claim that they met the system that way therefore it's not their fault that it is corrupt so there is nothing they can do about it. You will hear clichés like, 'it is a crime to be lawful in an unlawful society'. They might go as far as telling you that it cannot be changed and that any attempt to reform it even marginally will be a waste of time and all sort of discouraging tales. They will ask you to concentrate on 'making it', that is, achieving your primary dream anyhow you can by hook or by crook. Whatever is the collateral damage to that should not bother you.

They will tell you that after all, everybody does it, which is steals; that nobody is clean. Some listen to them and give up, while others listen to them and refuse to buy the crap. That is why we have men like Martin Luther King, Lee Kwan Yew, Mao Zedong, Abraham Lincoln, Charles de Gaulle, Winston Churchill, Nelson Mandela, Barrack Obama and other great reformers and leaders who have contributed a lot to re-make their society and in extension advance civilization because they rejected cynicism and refused to be discouraged. Where do you belong to in these four categorizations: i, ii, iii or iv?

108.   Your values determine the use to which you put your intellect, talent, reason, knowledge and skills.

109.   Any society that does not attach importance to values, ideas and knowledge as essential raw materials for development will be on a downward spiral and a continuous state of atrophy.

110.   It's a paradox that Nigerians, 99% of whom are adherents of religions that preach and teach the right values don't choose their leaders based on the right values. Their leaders, of which 99% are adherents of same religions that teach the right values don't lead them based on the right values. The leaders and the led are not authentic hence the disconnect between the two and the below average results that are on display.

111.   Do you want a nation where you are so rich through fraud and the people so poor and wretched or a nation where you are rich by legal means and opportunities for upward mobility abound for the people?

112.   We should make a substantial part of our intellect available for public benefit not personal gains alone because what makes us humans is that we are intelligent enough or have adequate intellectual reserve to think not only for ourselves but also for others.

113.   The perception seems to be that Nigerians are docile. I beg to disagree. Nigerians are one of the most boisterous, energetic, vibrant, active, proud and confident people on earth. Why we seem to be politically docile is because everyone is fighting for himself. When it comes to grabbing/ getting/ securing something or anything for themselves, you will see the vintage Nigerian in his elements; aggressive, die-hard, smart, tactful and ready to undermine the law and due process, jump queues, cut corners, lie, doctor vital documents including age declaration (birth registration in Nigeria is primeval) if he has a slight chance of getting away with it. In those days when I served, it is customary to see persons who are in their late thirties and early forties in National Youth Service Corps (NYSC) camps. We used to call them over age. These are people who doctored their date of birth, DOB, to make themselves eligible for service because the NYSC statute bars those who are above 30years. We feel very fulfilled when we achieve our goals the wrong way and can boast with it as a sign of our smartness and/ or connection/ contacts. Those of us who go to religious places won't boast much but will airbrush how we accomplished whatever it is that we achieved and give testimonies/ host thanksgivings about what God has done for us. We need to listen to our consciences and turn a better leaf.

114.   If this country must attain its full potential, the leadership of the country; politicians and public servants alike must stop the practice of using public offices for personal gains. Public offices must be used to serve the public interest; the national interest. Now, it is very important for us to realize that Nigeria is bigger than any individual. We should therefore respect the country than persons. Nigeria is "its people and their laws". Whoever disrespect the laws of this country disrespect this nation and its people and does not deserve our respect. Impunity, flouting or breaking our laws should be seen as spitting on our faces. Our security agencies should not be an appendage of the ruling party. Our laws, the laws of the land should deal with every lawbreaker. No one is greater than a society or community and we should not allow it. There must be equality before the law. We need to find a way to get the law to work because we can't depend on the magnanimity of politicians and public officers to do the right thing. We should depend on our laws to compel them to do the right thing.

115.   Assuming you are working with someone on a project; while you are putting in your best intellectually, physically and professionally to make it work and judge the success of the project by the achievement of deliverables to quality specifications; if your partner doesn't care about quality delivery, know that he is after what he can fraudulently get out of it and can't make any excellent or quality input into the project. If he is the one in charge of the project purse, won't he create circumstances that will enable him divert the project funds thereby jeopardizing the project? Therefore, when you are working on a project with someone and he is with the

project purse; if you realize that the person is not interested in quality or adherence to standards and specification, such a person is interested in something: what he will dishonestly get out of the project and you better be careful.

116.   Be wary of anyone you are dealing with, a friend or someone who might even profess the same faith with you, who is highly ambitious and greedy for money and or power. Someone who scorns morals, values and principles. Someone who argues that the end justifies the means. You should be cautious because it will be sheer foolishness for you to think that he will not use you as expendable if his warped reasoning tells him that so doing will help him achieve his selfish goals or ends.

117.   It is very important for each and every one of us to self-censor ourselves. We need to ask ourselves if whatever we are doing is ethical, moral or right. If it is not, then we desist forthwith. It is hypocritical for us to sit back and run our mouths about what people in government are doing wrong when in our little corners we do worse things. The leadership cohort that will take this country out of the woods must be that with a high moral and ethical standard. A disciplined and incorruptible leadership group. If you share in the vision of a great Nigerian nation and want to be a member of this leadership elite, you have to start building this high moral and ethical standard, this discipline and incorruptibility now through self-censorship and a personal commitment to doing the ethical, moral and right thing at all times whether it is convenient or not.

118. What are the lifestyles, values, mindsets, orientations, and mentality that have supported and sustained our inability to be where we ought to be (the pride of the black race all over the world)? What are the mores, mindsets, orientations, lifestyles and values we need to imbibe to achieve that manifest destiny?

119. In an environment where there is extreme poverty, the capacity of the people to get meaningfully involved in politics is highly restricted. It therefore follows that they can be swayed by food or money because they do not have a mind of their own. Poverty has eroded their dignity and free will. To get these people out of poverty will still be through the instrumentality of politics. However, the politics that will get them out of poverty will not be the petty kind of politics that take advantage of people's misfortune or incapacity but that which call on their best virtues: the virtues of faith, hope and hard work; the virtues of integrity, dignity and honesty.

120. The problem is not the lack of intelligence but the lack of values which make our leaders ineffective and hollow. They therefore cannot produce sustainable results because they are using their intelligence to see how they can feather their own nest not how they can develop the nation. They find it difficult to pay sustained attention to any scheme, project or programme that will not profit or benefit them. However, it is this sustained attention and commitment that is required to make projects work. Their pecuniary interests will not allow it. They are always looking to initiate new projects and take out their percentage. Whether the projects are completed

according to specification or not, they don't care because that is secondary to them or worse still none of their business. After all, no one will call them to account.

121.   As a young man growing up, I had a lot of wonderful ideas on how the society can be transformed. I tried to partner with people whose public posturing was that of reformers and progressives. I realized when I got closer that a lot of people who are politically exposed and seem to be financially buoyant achieved and still sustain their economic relevance by engaging in acts (such as getting contracts by greasing palms among others) that need to be phased out or punished if the country must progress. Because their sources of livelihood and leisure are faulty, they are compromised and are actually part of the problem they stridently speak against and pose as having solutions to. Working with people like that is a complete waste of time and there are many of them around. In fact, 90 percent of politicians and businessmen fall into this category. Consequently, young people who want to make a difference politically should realize that it is a tough call that will require them to create and follow a different path rather than queue behind empty vessels who have lost their path and missed the way even though they carry big tags of being past this and former that; current this and present that.

122.   Young people need mentors and role models. Unfortunately here, anyone mentoring you in politics is likely to teach you how to manipulate people and the electoral process; not how to identify the needs of the people, conceptualize policies and programmes to address those needs, sell them to the electorates to win their

support, get their votes and provide good governance when elected so as to earn their trust and goodwill. You must involve yourself in one form of electoral misconduct or the other if you must be in their good books and be considered a worthy protégé. Anyone mentoring you in business here is likely to teach you how to give bribes to get ahead if he does business with government. They are likely to teach you how to visit government officials to negotiate for projects and contracts not how to be proficient in tender or bid preparation and presentation. In choosing your mentor, let the right values be your guide.

123.   The desire to be rich and wealthy is not bad. The issue is; how do you intend to make it? What ideas do you have in your head? Is it stealing, cheating, smuggling and killing to conceal your path if necessary or the development of world class products and services?

124.   Our politics is rooted in the conflicts of personal interest cloaked in regional, tribal or ethnic gowns. It revolves around cake sharing rather than cake baking. Most Nigerian politicians who have anything to offer have been compromised or overwhelmed by the occasion due to lack of guiding principles, values and codes of ethics. It pays for a politician to have a big vision, focus on the big picture and stay the course despite the hostilities; consistency pays.

125.   Most of the time, we might not know what we should do; however, it is very important for us to know what we should not do. That's the nature of common law. It tells us mostly what we should not do. Therefore, what we should not do becomes a guide to morality and getting

it right because what we should not do is a codification of very harmful and dangerous stuffs that will set the society and system back when we do them. When in doubt – learn what you should not do – and abide by them for the general good.

126.   The expectation on our political leaders and public officers by their immediate constituency is personal not societal or communal. Their performance is judged by those who are close to them (their family, circle of friends, party members' et al who really matter in their lives and form their social support structure) based on how the politician and public officer has affected or touched their lives economically and financially (they don't care if this is done in a manner that negates the law and laid down rules and regulations which is detrimental to the society). Those who expect a public officer to 'perform' (for the gain of the society and nation) are those who are not close to him (those who don't know him personally so to say). Those who know him expect him to perform for their personal gains and benefits by doling out cash to them; giving them jobs and appointments and awarding contracts to them and other favors without following laid down rules and regulations. The act of using political offices as tools for dispensing favors and for personal gains are at the root of corruption in our society. Most of our ills can be attributed to our societal sub-structure, values, reward systems and expectation framework. If our political office holders have no family, friends, religious organisations and peers (social clubs, parties) to exert negative pressures and influences on them; they will shine like a million stars.

127.   We need a guiding philosophy anchored by a set of common national values to help us navigate the ocean of challenges surrounding our nation so as to arrive at the shore of internal peace and sustainable development.

128.   We should emphasize more on ethics, discipline, honesty, hard work, integrity, and the right values as the cornerstone or foundation for the nation's rapid social, political and economic development. Our reward system should reflect and emphasize that. Without a strong social infrastructure as a base, we are building on a weak foundation. The integrity of what we build should be as important as what we are building.

129.   We have the challenge of constructing a national identity – shared core values – beyond religious or ethnic identities. We have the challenge of promoting a shared vision which Nigerians of different ethnic stock, languages and other diversities will subscribe to.

130.   If everyone in Nigeria is living exactly the same way you are living, thinking exactly the same way you are thinking, doing exactly the same things you are doing; would our country be getting progressively better or worse?

131.   If you don't feel a strong demand for discipline on you; you are not a leader but a mere title holder whose accomplishments can never be first rated, untarnished and unblemished. This is because discipline is the key to producing extra-ordinary results.

132.   The speed at which the country is moving on the expressway of impunity and indiscipline creates a creepy feeling that if men of honor and excellence remain quiet, Nigeria might become a country where people go to prison for not giving bribes as against being a country where people go to jail for giving bribes.

133.   One of the reasons why Nigeria has so many bright minds and educated citizens resident in the country and in almost every part of the world but is still trapped in mediocrity and backwardness is because a great many of them are pursuing wrong causes represented by sectional and personal interests. This might be as a result of the fact that there is no clear national interest to identify with because it is vague, undefined or probably non-existent. We therefore need to define what the national interest is beyond indivisibility since indivisibility is not a source of pride, dignity and respect. In my opinion, answering the question; 'what is the purpose of Nigeria and how do we intend to achieve that purpose?' is the beginning of conceptualizing a national interest that will captivate Nigerians and engender patriotism and pride for the motherland.

134.   We should develop a culture, tradition or value system that esteem a janitor, driver or steward with integrity, values, good morals and sound principles more than a president, minister, senator or governor without integrity. A culture or tradition which regards anyone who doesn't have the right values and principles as a non-entity or a persona non grata.

CHAPTER SIX
Right Orientation

135.   It is very important for us to note that we are coming from decades of military dictatorship characterized by might is right; divide and rule; the suspension of constitutional order; rule by decrees issued by a few avaricious men; the coercion, forceful conscription and compromise of the responsible section of our political and business elite to destroy their credibility and make them susceptible to manipulation; and many other ills. Most players in government today became prominent and grew through the ranks during the military era when there was no competition; the criteria for advancement was not strictly based on merit but on the willingness to do the bidding of military masters whether good or bad, right or wrong; no accountability; shady and underhand deals went unchallenged. Now that we have civil rule, we need to dethrone this culture and the people who are still stuck to it. We need to roll back civilian dictatorship and advance the frontiers of democracy.

136.   Many of our political leaders and public servants view government projects as an opportunity to make money. Once they take out what they want, the project or programme can succeed or die and most often, it dies because there is no genuine interest to ensure it succeeds. There was no sustainability plan from the outset. It was not set up to last but to take out money through kickbacks.

137.   After eating and drinking, it seems we expend more energy on singing and dancing across our social strata — from the villages to the cities, from the

countryside to urban areas – than spare a little time for deep thinking, logical reasoning and sound intellectual exploration which lead to objectivity, correct judgment, good decision making and right choices. That is why in a constitutional democracy guided by laws enacted by the legislative arm of government, the governor of a certain state – with or without listening to himself – can stand in a gathering and say emphatically like a kingmaker (a position not recognized by democracy) that everybody can contest an election but that the winner will come from a certain geographical or ethnic enclave and the audience will applaud him. How will he achieve that boast if not by manipulating the electoral process in his state during general elections? As if that was not enough, he prayed for the audience and they chorused Amen! Some supported the governor's view by parroting that democracy is all about justice and fairness therefore the governorship position should go around. A stand not supported by their laws or constitution of the land. Where is the electorate in all these avowals? They forget that the basic tenet of democracy is 'one man, one vote'. What kind of justice do they want to achieve with election rigging which is illegal? What kind of fairness do they want to achieve with electoral malpractices which is unlawful? It is ironic that the said governor and the audience believe in God but are not interested in the admonition about abiding by the laws of their land which proscribes and criminalizes election rigging or His position about breaking the laws contained in the scriptures they copiously quote. They really don't care about His admonitions like the golden rule which asks them to "do unto others as you want them to do unto you" which in this case is:

If you won't be happy if someone rigs an election you clearly won so that you become the loser after all your efforts in time and expenses in resources on the campaign trail, don't do it to others. What a people? They believe in praying to God to make their country good, but they don't believe in doing what God asked them to do for their country to be good. The fact is that until we begin to put the greatest resource God has given us which is our brain and thinking faculty into good and proper use, we will keep running around in circles; claiming that we are developing while we are not advancing intellectually, morally and socially which in themselves are the keystones of development.

138.   Have a solution mindset, not a daily bread or need mindset. If you have a solution mindset, you will be committed to making a living by solving problems while ensuring that you don't create or involve yourself in anything that will create more problems. If you have a daily bread or need mindset, you will be committed to making a living by hook or by crook, by means fair or foul; by solving problems or creating problems whichever one will do; whichever one is convenient; whichever one you have to do to satisfy your daily need as quickly and as fast as possible. This is because the only thing that is a problem to someone who is driven by his daily bread or needs is his stomach or desperations. If it is satisfied, then all is well no matter how it is mollified.

139.   You are politically relevant when you have ideas and your political group or party is implementing those ideas. You are politically relevant when your beliefs are in sync with that of your political party. You are politically relevant when the manifesto of the party which you

believe in is being vigorously implemented. You are politically relevant when your political group or party believe in internal party democracy and in aggregating the views of its members before reaching a decision.

140.	We should deal on general principles and ideas on what we need to do to make the system work efficiently for the good of all. Our reference point for judging politicians' performance in office should be scientific not subjective. The geographical or ethnic origin of a local government chairman, senator, governor or the president should therefore not be an issue. We should realize by now that it is an emotional and sentimental pursuit that will lead us nowhere. The quality of the candidate should be the primary focus.

141.	The essence of a country is people coming together to pursue common goals. Nigeria seems not to be exhibiting the characteristics of a country in the real sense of the word because it is a republic in perpetual petty conflicts at the expense of its economy and society. It seems we have come together so that everyone, most especially politicians, can pursue their personal goals at the expense of the whole, the society, the nation. This they do by hiding under the cover and canopy of their hamlets, tribes and ethnic groups, religions and regions – geography or bush – to con and deceive. They con and deceive the gullible, the consenting, the tribalistic, the parochial, the narrow minded, the fanatical and the mentally lazy in the name of ruses like fighting for their rights or representing their ethnic, regional or religious interests.

142.   For many, as far as they are getting what they want for themselves in the country by hook or by crook; everything is fine. This is without considering the fact that 70% of 160million of their countrymen are wallowing in creepy abject poverty and that the number of poor people keep going up with increase in GDP because of their hook and crook.

143.   In my view, I don't think it is entirely correct for anyone to say that bad governance is not a causative factor for Boko Haram. The accusation that they want to establish an Islamic state does not support such assertion. Why would anyone want to establish an Islamic state? Probably because they feel that it's a state where there will be justice and in extension justice will mean that there will be less poverty. The war against the Boko Haram terrorists' group is an ideological war with economic roots. In essence, Boko Haram might have been thrown up by economic deprivation. Lack of good governance is therefore a causative factor. In any case, assuming that lack of good governance is not a causative factor, – even though we will eventually defeat Boko Haram because they are non-state actors – bad governance has definitely made efforts aimed at routing them long drawn and protracted. For instance, in the absence of any official response to the Daily Sun editorial of April 28, 2014 titled 'Probe the Abuja CCTV Project'; how else can one explain the bungling of a N76 billion ($420 million) project which would have helped the cause of fighting the Boko Haram menace and the provision of adequate security in the cities of Abuja and Lagos if not bad governance?

144.   Most of our problems are ethics and values related and can be traced to the erosion of our value system due to unbridled materialism and greed. Many active politicians in Nigeria joined politics to make money. They therefore see it as a money-making venture and route to quick riches. This has led to the distortion of due process and laid down rules and regulations. Our ideal is supposed to be the laws that we have not made but at present, the laws that we have which is supposed to be our reality is now our ideal. Our present reality is impunity, disrespect for due process as well as laid down rules and regulations and lack of proactive and diligent law enforcement. It's a fool's errand and illusion to expect a transformational change that does not start from changing our values most especially that of politicians whose footsteps the people always imitate.

145.   In recent times, it seems as if Nigerians have developed a very high personal economic brilliance but low socio-economic intelligence; a high level of family and tribe intelligence quotient (IQ) but a very low level of communal and national intelligence quotient (IQ).

146.   Our current development expectation is built on a faulty, false and fake foundation (of impunity, indiscipline, disdain for due process, abuse of rules and regulations, legal breaches etc.) which we call 'the Nigerian' factor or 'the reality'. Can we attain our development goals without addressing these retrogressive tendencies?

147.   One of the problems we have with governance in Nigeria is that of concept. The concept of politics and governance just need to be redefined in a very

fundamental way. This redefinition of concept will help change our psychology and orientation about politics and governance in a very profound manner for all-encompassing result. For I reckon that we need revolution in Nigeria, albeit a mental, ethical and social revolution. However, mental or psychological revolution is the key because it precedes moral and social revolution. Experts in human behaviours believe that personal and social changes (new and better approach of doing things) involve mental revolution – change in mode of thinking, belief and values. In Nigeria's case, mental revolution involves changing our mindset, psychology and orientation about government. It involves having a proper understanding of the purpose of government and seeking to align our actions for the achievement of that purpose. Presently, the fact and the truth are that many Nigerians regard stealing government money as normal when they are on the sharing table and abnormal when they are not on the sharing table. This is a mode of thinking or orientation I have seen play out even as a kid growing up in the late 80s and early 90s.

In my teen, during the military days and before the advent of democracy in 1999; I have encountered a much-respected member of a church who claims to be a politician, someone in the league of knights, with no farmland gather people who equally have no farms to scheme for and obtain agricultural loans from government which they never pay back. This is done as freely as drinking water, with happiness, laughter and no remorse at all. Over the years, this sort of practice and other variants of it have not changed but have rather increased in leaps and bounds and become more sophisticated and widespread. Almost everyone in the corridors of power is out to enrich himself. The orientation and psychology are that there is nothing wrong about stealing government money even though we collectively denounce government officials and politicians caught stealing once in a while. These government officials and politicians caught stealing know that our expression of disgust and disapproval border on hypocrisy so they are not really bothered. The society is not ready for change so what, they say to themselves. They believe that those shouting and hurling insults at them will do worse than them if they find themselves in the same position; so, it's all sham and grandstanding. The society validates the stealing of government money by their actions. They besiege the politician or public officer's house in their hundreds seeking for money. Where do they want him to get it from? When did he become the social security officer of the Nigerian state? If he doesn't give them, they will regard him as being wicked. Governance in Nigeria therefore seems to have become organized stealing. The leaders and the led are complicit. The evidence abounds but sometimes we don't want to admit it. We kind of feel that somehow, we shall get ahead and achieve socio-economic progress nonetheless. What a delusion?

In this country, hardly any government contract is awarded, completed and duly paid for without some politicians or public officers' pockets being heavily greased. What is the way forward for Nigeria then? The way forward is for Nigerians to come to terms with the fact that stealing government money by them or anyone is wrong and should be strictly punished. Who should catch offenders? The police of course! In the Nigerian police for instance, the completion certificate of a typical police building project in a state which will be paid for in Abuja is signed by; i). The state's works officer ii). The zonal works officer iii). The commissioner of police and iv). The assistant inspector general of police. Should these four public officers extort money from a contractor before appending their signatures on a completion certificate? No. If they shouldn't and they do, how then do we expect the police to arrest official stealing, bribery and corruption in Nigeria when the officers charged with that responsibility are neck deep in the act? I still believe we can if for a start, we adopt the concept that government houses are not cash centers and agree that official stealing, bribery and corruption is wrong; should be uprooted and be resolute in our stand.

148.   If you are a politician and you don't understand how business works; what then is your business in politics? In fact, you have no business being in politics. Businesses develop products and services; businesses employ people, businesses create wealth. Your primary reason for being in politics should be to help create conditions that will allow businesses to thrive and you can't do this effectively if you don't know how business work or should work. So, get the knowledge.

149.   Political talks around Nigerian communities revolve around personalities and the sharing of the spoils of public office. Government is primarily judged by how many from one's constituency have appointments and jobs. Even when infrastructures come, it is still evaluated based on whether the contract was awarded to a member of that community. This is wrong!

150.   Many Nigerians "mentally and morally famished by poverty on one hand, and mentally and morally bankrupt

by greed on the other" don't organize and position themselves to add or contribute to the system for societal, communal, national or general good but to extract from the system for their own personal and selfish benefits.

151.   Our present democracy seems to exist to service the needs of the elite class who parade as contractors and consultants. The challenge we face is making democracy work for the common man. What shall we do to make democracy stop working for the elites alone and start working for the common man also? Ensuring free and fair election is a good start.

152.   At the moment, Nigerian politics is not dominated by gifted and humble people who believe in production and productivity, who owns means of production and have faith in the market to survive in business. But rather, our politics is dominated by greedy and proud people who don't understand production, who owns means of extraction and depend on their connection with people in power or government – not the market – to succeed.

153.   There is a perspective that to be a lawful citizen in a lawless society is a crime. My counter perspective is that working towards making a lawless society lawful is a noble cause. Which one do you subscribe to?

154.   The fact that most ordinary people we consider unreasonable or unsound will behave well and fit into organized societies suggests that there is a relationship between the environment and behavior; a relationship between culture, tradition and psychology.

155.   People who love their country can change it.

156.   We should not celebrate people for the money they have but for the value they create or add to the society.

157.   Knowing your culture or root – your cultural department in the world – gives you the foundation and frame of reference you need to relate well with people from other cultures respectfully and contribute to the betterment and advancement of human civilization, starting from your culture or root.

158.   Your political leader should be someone from your ideological conclave, not someone from your geological enclave. Likewise, your political followership should be people from your ideological conclave, not people from your geographical enclave.

159.   "God said to build a better world and I said how? The world is such a cold, dark place and so complicated now; and I'm so young and useless there is nothing I can do. But God, in all his wisdom said, 'just build a better you'" - Anon. Building a better you is the first step to building a better Nigeria. The solution starts with you and if everyone becomes part of the solution, Nigeria will be able to swiftly tackle its numerous manmade problems.

CHAPTER SEVEN
Common Sense Issues

160.   I'm very skeptical about religious claims, platitudes and calls to prayer as the solution to Nigeria's problems. I believe we need to pray and in the same breath; Nigerians should be made to know that it doesn't end there. They should be made to know that we need good thinking (the use of our intellect), hard work and a good dose of integrity to come out of the woods. Prayers do help the nation because it builds up our spiritual and in extension our social lives. However, it doesn't formulate good government policies and programmes; maintain law and order; establish and sustain systems and institutions etcetera. The intelligent, ethical and diligent deployment of scientific knowledge does.

161.   The silver bullet for eliminating corruption from public and private life in Nigeria might be; i. to place the burden of proof on the accused in the case of financial corruption and ii. Establishing special courts to try corruption cases.

162.   If we give our common sense a chance, we will realize that tolerance is Godliness. If God allowed people we view from the eyes of our religions to be infidels, sinners, unbelievers and other qualifying adjectives to live and even prosper in their chosen careers according to the natural law of sowing and reaping, why should we be the ones to make life difficult for them — people God has afforded the good things of nature and life? The scriptures of our religions even admonish us to show love to people

who don't believe what we believe and treat them kindly. We all share the same humanity and what is consistent about nature is diversity. That is why we have different kinds of the same species: Different kinds of butterflies; different colors of roses; different kinds of fishes in the river, seas and oceans; different kinds of birds; different kinds of goats; different kinds of dogs; different kinds of almost everything except perhaps, the sun and the moon in our galaxy. Therefore, life is all about diversity and heterogeneity. We should learn to accept nature the way we see it and stop trying to turn it into what we think it should be. It's an impossible task, a mission destined to fail and a sheer waste of time and energy. It is said that you can't cheat nature; I dare say that you can't change it. Accept people who are different than or from you in color, culture, religion et al the way you have accepted day and night, sunshine and rain, summer and winter. Accept them the way you have accepted the diversity of nature so that we can live in peace.

We should not only view serving God in the light of our religion as proselytizing but also as allowing what we believe to affect the way we think and the way we relate with people. If our relationship with people brings them discomfort, it is either something is wrong with us or with the way we understand and practice our religion or both. Yes, if our relationship with people who do not profess our religion brings them serious discomfort and dislocation, we need to evaluate ourselves or the way we understand our religion.

163.   Any nation built on religion is an artificial creation. It will have internal contradictions as a result of its conflict with the natural law of diversity. No society is purely

homogenous and none can be. Every religion has diversities which manifest in sects that don't agree about fundamental issues in their religion. Islam has sects: the Sunni, the Shiite, the Alawites and others. Christianity has sects: the Catholics, the Protestants and others. Which sect will a religious society uphold without being unfair, unjust and dictatorial - attributes that does not belong to the God of any known religion? Every religious text recognizes that there are others and advises its adherents on how to treat devotees of other religion. No religion has prescriptions for the form of government a society should have. The form of government in a society is the creation of fallible men. It is therefore an aberration for men to build societies, governments or nations on religion and clothe it with Divinity. It's a recipe for intolerance which breeds strife or false peace sustained with the instrument of fear, terror and intimidation. Any society or nation that craves for true peace, stability and social harmony must not make laws based on any particular religious belief but on the principles of natural justice.

164.   Common sense tells us that if a people are honest and have integrity, they can, with the agency of the intellect, logic, reason and knowledge transform or change their society for good. They often don't make decisions only for their personal benefits. They are not looking after their own interest alone. They look after the interest of the community and take decisions that will benefit the society even if it causes them some personal losses. They look ahead and make plans for generations yet unborn.

165.   A governor was once reported to have sustained a minor head injury in an accident and was flown overseas

for treatment. Why did he not subject himself to be treated in the health centers he has purportedly built and or equipped for his people or the ones his 35 other colleagues have built and equipped in their states assuming he is yet to do that? Is he not one of the people? Is his ailment or accident different from the ones thousands of his people contract or encounter every day? Doesn't this suggest that the projects are not good enough? If so, do any of those governors have the moral right to (or on what basis do any of these governors) market to us as achievements - hospitals they and their families don't patronize and schools their children can't attend? I think we are not discerning when we celebrate these shams as achievements or democracy dividends. Our journalists are the guiltier probably because they get brown envelopes. They are fond of eulogizing these governors and their so-called development strides which are often followed up with bogus and dubious awards of 'man of the year', 'politicians of the year', 'best governor in this or that'. Is it extremism to insist that no governor can be said to be achieving or to have achieved anything in the education sector if his children and the children of his commissioners, party chairmen and executives, advisers, legislators and other government functionaries cannot attend or are not attending the public schools he or they have built? It is high time we stop spreading, encouraging and cuddling mediocrity.

166.   It bothers me when some Nigerians over-celebrate and make too much noise about things we are just doing now, which people in other climes have done or achieved 200 years ago. Great Britain built the London underground system about 150 years ago. We have none at the

moment. Should we build one in ten- or twenty-years' time perhaps with foreign technology and expertise, we will make so much noise about it as if we have done what has never been done anywhere in the world or achieved something spectacular. The question is; agreed that the people will benefit from the infrastructural project, what is really spectacular about them. Is it that they were initiated, designed and executed by indigenous engineers? Is it that the materials used to construct them were locally sourced? Is it that the technology used to build them was locally invented and therefore will not require additional maintenance expense for many years?

Is it that very soon, people will come from all over the world to enquire about how we managed to get this project done because this is the only place it has been done in the world? Is it that the cost of the project is by a great factor less than a conventional one? That is, there is a significant cost saving arising from the methodology used by the state to award and manage the contract? The question is; what really is spectacular about these projects that we make so much noise about? What feat has been achieved that is uncommon, groundbreaking or revolutionary? It is rather unfortunate that we seem to have reduced the serious art of governance to casting bridges and culverts with the attendant parties and ceremonies organized around them.

167.   It is a tragedy when people who have limited knowledge and are not willing to add to that knowledge; strongly and seriously seek to be leaders and decision makers in fields that require vast expert knowledge, while

those who have the knowledge in these fields are passive about becoming leaders and decision makers.

168.   We should be very mindful of the result we want. At this moment, there is no need denigrating or speaking ill of any past leader because that won't solve any problem. Instead, it will lead to unnecessary controversies, mudslinging and distractions. Agreed we have a right not to be happy with some of their actions in the past, we have to concede however that they could only give what they had. The mistakes they made will now serve as a guide and compass for us. A guide on what we should do and should not do. I think that's the positives we should take from their actions. Though we may rightly accuse them of lacking foresight, we should not be guilty of lacking hindsight.

169.   The National Assembly should come up with a legislation on indigenization that will allow any Nigerian to vie for election in any state where he has lived and paid tax for ten years and define indigenization as the right to indigenous ownership of land which will really help us to deal with the problem of tribalism/ethnicity. People are incited by their feckless elites to clamor for 'their own' to be elected because they, the kingmakers and political elites, see political office as a platform to dispense favors to themselves and therefore do not want 'outsiders' to be part of it (sharing the booty). They, 'outsiders' should go to their places of 'origin' and share their people's cake not 'our people's cake.' Political office is not seen as a platform for service or sacrifices for societal development but as a platform for corrupt enrichment for those who capture power.

170.   One of the most important lessons I have learnt as a social and political observer is that to succeed as an aspiring politician, you need to come into your own economically so that you can secure the independence you need to stand steadfastly behind your ideas and push it through; make the right kind of friends, establish the right kind of partnership and forge the right kind of alliances that will enable you to achieve your political goals and dreams without compromising your principles and values for economic reasons.

171.   The greatest force on earth is men and women working together in unison with the same focus, direction, vision and goal. The law is a representation or expression of that agreement. Agreement on broad outlines about what should be done and what should not be done and an attempt to ensure that everyone is whipped into line when they try to deviate. Any society where law enforcement is not taken as a serious business will be disorganized and chaotic.

172.   The crisis on our hands means that we truly have a lot of work to do. We need to look for tools and inputs, knowledge and skills, that will enable us get these works done. At the moment, there is no aspect of our national life that is working optimally. Education, Health, Housing, Utility, Security, Sports and others. Is it that the knowledge and skills necessary to solve these problems or tackle these challenges are not there? Is it that we have the tools, the knowledge, the skills, and the manpower but lack a sense of duty, responsibility and commitment necessary to get the work done?

173.   We need to be more deliberative and place premium on knowledge as the key to unlocking knotty issues and solving problems. We should therefore understand that it is very important for us to have 'adequate' knowledge about a situation or problem and identify the information, skills and competencies required to get it solved. This will enable us to mobilize resources in 'complete measure' to get the problem solved satisfactorily rather than be involved in so many things and be expert at nothing.

174.   Inasmuch as we look back at past years in the life of our nation and realize that we don't have much to cheer about, those past years however are not altogether a failure or waste after all. This is because it gave us an experiential knowledge and insight into what ought not to be done. The confidence we have in condemning certain ways of doing things stem from the facts we have from history to support our stand that those ways of doing things did not work, is not working and will never work. Whatever new theory or awareness we possess about the way things should be done has these past failures as raw materials. Therefore, in speaking about the past, analyzing the past and the people that drove the process, we have to do so with humility.

175.   No one can have life, liberty or the possibility of happiness unless his country is alive, free and happy –
Dorothy Thompson

176.   Education is human capital development while health is the maintenance and sustenance of human

capital. Good educational and health policies are very essential to the development of any nation.

177.   Our educational system is anchored on the wrong philosophy of graduating from school as a passport to advancing in life. The skills and knowledge components are subdued. We need to know that everybody has talents and gifts and that our educational system should enable them find and develop their talents to the full.

178.   If we can change our work ethics, half of our problems will be solved. People should have a sense of duty and responsibility. The teacher should teach well, the nurse should nurse well; the chef should cook well - in compliance with the ethics of their professions. This will need a push from the center and should be part of a cultural transformation and orientation needed to move the country forward.

179.   The best way to succeed as a young person starting out on the road to achieving lofty dreams and aspirations and make time your best friend is to domicile most of what has to be done for you to achieve success within you, hang in there and grind it out. If most of what has to be done for you to achieve success is dependent on others, you must be very sure of the character, moral and ethical strength of such people. If you don't, you will unfortunately wake up some time in the future to realize that you have wasted years by building your castle in the air, falsehood or deceit. You may regrettably find out after some years have gone by that they were not fulfilling their own part of the bargain but have been leading you on all along with the impression that they are with you. You may

painfully find out that they have never been on the same page with you most especially if their input to the project or assignment requires ethical and moral discipline on their part. Therefore, don't judge people based on titles, past achievements, profiles or reputations spurned in the press. Select your mentors or people to entrust important responsibilities for the realization of your vision carefully. Choose them based on personal experience working on tasks with them or based on thorough background checks and very credible references. This is very necessary because despite our public show of religious piety, the population of defeated men and women who have lost the battle of morals, ethics and values in this clime is very high. If you take things for granted, they will mess you up.

180.   There are noble values that are natural to Nigeria: Freedom of speech; freedom of association; and freedom of worship. They are entrenched here as the dominant culture and norm and we work daily to deepen and expand their reach. Governments and groups that have tried to undermine them always find themselves on the wrong side of public opinion, fishing in dangerous waters or swimming against the tide.

CHAPTER EIGHT

Economic Matters

181.   We need to produce more of the things we consume and consume more of the things we produce.

182.   We have the challenge of service and product quality. The Nigerian government agencies responsible for quality assurance are moribund. They don't have funds for operations while legislators are paid obscene wages for providing social services that can be done part-time with minimal expenses. The vision, motivation and priorities of our political elites are questionable. I think we lack a basic understanding of what the functions, purposes and responsibilities of government are. What is government and what are its basic functions? The answer is to provide for the security and welfare of its citizens. If we can spend more than a trillion naira on legislators in 10 years, we don't have any excuse for not adequately funding our quality enforcement and assurance agencies. We need to fund them to adequately carry out their functions of ensuring that the services we offer and get; the goods we produce or import for sale meets global quality standards and specifications at all times. Our markets should not accommodate a high- and low-quality variant of the same product at any time. This will promote Nigerian industry and exports thereby creating more wealth and quality jobs for quality living.

183.   Before anyone start employing people, shouldn't he or she obtain an employer identification number (EIN) to be issued by the Ministry of Labor and Productivity? The purpose should be to know the number of Nigerians who

are employed and their salaries for record purposes and for planning. Besides, the Nigerian state, like any other state has to protect its citizens. A government should not leave its citizens, the workforce at the mercy of greedy, wicked and unscrupulous employers who maintain ostentatious lifestyles while they simultaneously underpay their workers and/or owe their workers' salaries for many months.

184.   Alan Greenspan was reported to contend that globalization (has a disinflationary effect) plays a role in keeping inflation down. IMF staffers also agreed. Does the Central Bank of Nigeria agree with this view? Then it has to loosen monetary policy, work with the Federal Ministry of Finance to reduce custom duties to allow for the importation of more goods to meet increase in demand in the medium term. The loose monetary policy will increase access to credit to MSMEs for growth and improved industrial output. Increased industrial output should result in gradual rise in custom duties so that locally produced goods – made cheaper by access to low interest loans – can fill in the supply gap. The present tight monetary policy which translates to high interest rate surely hurts investment in the real sector of the economy as well as employment generation.

185.   Development and economic growth are traditionally driven by government investment and household consumption. What is Nigeria's growth model and what are the economic fundamentals that will underpin employment generating growth?

What should Nigeria's Growth Model be?

Our growth model should be investing in infrastructures and human capital development. Promoting policies that will liberalize the economy and promote private, local and foreign investment in industries that will produce primarily to meet local demand. This will establish the framework for an economy that will be dependent on local demand to grow in the long run. This will however not preclude investments and the promotion of policies that will push up exports in sectors we have comparative advantage to produce for the world.

186.   To promote Nigerian industry and manufacturing, we can begin by encouraging our artisans to adopt or commit to high quality standards and evolve means of ensuring that they do so. We should regulate every industry to ensure that those engaged in it have the license which comes after training, certification and induction to practice it. That way, we enhance industry skill and expert knowledge base.

187.   If we must engender the culture of product quality and excellence in service delivery; we should not tolerate mediocrity, settle for less than we deserve, manage poor job or services. We must be demanding as customers or consumers.

188.   There are lifestyles and mindsets that aid capitalism and promote capital formation. There are lifestyles and mindsets that promote entrepreneurship and job creation. If we don't have a made in Nigerian predisposition, how do we expect jobs to be created? Our tastes are too foreign and exotic. This has to change.

189.   We need development policies that are original; which internalize indigenous wisdom, knowledge, tradition and culture. We need to find a way to help our people to be more productive in the economic activities they know how to do best like fishing, farming, herbal medicine, food storage, trading and others. Also, we need to look at how we can industrialize and commercialize some of these economically viable activities. We need a system that is rooted in the culture and tradition of our people and their values. How did our society provide for its need for food, shelter and clothing? Did they have to import to meet those needs and by how much? What percentage of those needs are we presently providing for through importation? What percentage can we profitably meet through local production using mostly local inputs? How did they provide for security, maintain law and order, punish criminals and reward good behavior? What were the social systems and structures that created peaceful and content societies before the advent of contemporary forms of government? How can we identify, refine, remodel, modernize and mainstream them for development?

190.   We should make things and make them well; We should produce things and produce them well; We should grow things and grow them well; We should establish things and make them last.

CHAPTER NINE
The Nigeria Of My Dream

191.   The nation of my dream: A country where you are sure of your safety; where you are sure that your human and legal rights will be respected; where you are sure to get justice in a court of law and in good time too; where equal opportunity is guaranteed; a country where you will not face discrimination and persecution as a result of your faith, philosophy of life, and political leaning.

192.   I dream of a country where excellence is taken for granted. A country where the primary pursuit of its citizens is excellence - excellence first, other things second. A country where the pursuit of excellence is ingrained in our DNA and is one of our national values, ethos and watchword.

193.   The fact that we conducted a free and fair election in 1993 proves that a free and fair poll is possible in Nigeria. Not only that, it also indicates that we can do things right if we put our mind to it and see it as what we must do if we must progress. We have the capacity to get it right if we demonstrate enough will not wishes. We can be the best. We can do good things. We can do great things. We can do excellent things. We can do worthy things. If we will, not wish - we can make the quality of our health and educational systems one of the best in the world. If we will, not wish – we can make our civil service one of the most efficient in the world in service delivery. If we will, not wish - we can pave thousands of kilometers of federal, state and local government roads within a budget

year. If we will, not wish - we can establish the right structures for water and gas supplies to homes and industries just as we have done for power and telecoms. If we will, not wish - we can make sure that where possible, every square meter of this country's vast expanse of land is surveyed and planned to make provisions for agriculture, industrial layouts, grazing reserves, cities and estates – in fact to ensure that nobody in any part of this country puts up a structure in an area that has no plan to avoid the wastage of resources on demolition and the increasing multiplication of unplanned settlements and ghettos in many parts of the country even in the FCT. If we will, not wish - we can crown these with achieving order, peace and security in the society which are of great importance.

194.   Ethnic, regional or religious groupings aside, Nigeria consist of 'human beings' living in different parts of the country. We need a nation where everybody, no matter where they live have equal access and opportunities for self-advancement, development and fulfillment without any form of discrimination based on religion, political persuasion or ethnic stock. We should begin to see our ethnic group as a form of culture, tradition or art – the cultural department we belong to in Nigeria and stop using it as a basis for political mobilization or tool for political engagement. We should rather promote our culture as a form of art for the purpose of tourism, relaxation and entertainment and face politics based on issues that affect us all equally – common issues of justice, equal opportunity, security, education, healthcare and others.

195.   Setting an agenda for the political class: What are the features of an organized society? The task we should give our political leaders is the simple task of organizing the society. This means that we should develop the ideals and features of an organized society; determine where our society stand or score in the ideals and features and develop a roadmap of what we need to do to get organized with measurable parameters/indicators that will enable us judge/determine how far we have gone or the success/progress we are making in achieving those indices nay the status of an organized society.

196.   Is Nigeria a Christian, Islamic, Animist or Atheist nation? No! Nigeria is an open and free society. It is not an Islamic, Christian, Animist or Humanist nation but a nation of Muslims, Christians, Animists and Agnostics. More than 98% of Nigerians believe in God. This therefore presupposes, as constitutionally provided for, that anybody who is from any part of the geography called Nigeria has the right to settle in any part of the Nigerian topography of his choice, carry out his or her business, marry, own properties or assets and freely practice his religion without fear. Consequently, it is the responsibility of all our constitutionally recognized 774 local governments, 36 states, the federal capital territory (FCT) and the federal government to ensure that all Nigerian citizens and residents in their various territorial spheres of influence are free to fulfill their social, economic and spiritual purposes without molestation, threat, intimidation or harm.

197.   I dream of a nation of people who understand that their actions have consequences for the environment and

the society and are very conscious and aware of those that are negative and have the moral strength, character and values to resist what is wrong (like dumping refuse on the road and opening their sewer onto the street since the public health arms of local governments that are supposed to enforce sanitary laws only exist in name) and do the right thing no matter the cost. Doing the right thing will require effort from us and sometimes discomfort but when we look back and see the results, it can be very gratifying and satisfying and a source of pride.

198.   My vision is for Nigeria to be known as a nation of honest, happy and hardworking people who believe in God and in themselves. A nation of people who believe that their destiny is to be rich and prosperous and that as long as they are dedicated and diligent in their vocations, with a little patience; they shall be wealthy, successful and fulfilled.

199.   My hope in a greater Nigeria is informed by the fact that Nigeria has a lot of good people and you are one of them. Are you not? If you are, then you have every reason to believe that Nigeria will rise and be willing and ready to play your part as a citizen. The organized countries of the world some of us dream of travelling to are made so by the conscientious and sacrificial actions of their citizens.

200.   I dream of a nation whose economic development strategy is anchored on effective human capital development and mobilization. A nation that harnesses and makes optimum use of its vast human resources. A

nation that brings out the very best in its people and encourages them to attain their full potential.

INDEX

(PIB)., 30

A

A leader, *13*, *15*
A minister, *16*
accountability, 17,
19, 40, 48, 66,
72, 73, 90
appointments, 17,
21, 70, 87, 99

B

basic necessities,
31
blackmail, 34
Boko Haram, 21,
38, 94
businessman, 25,
54, 67

C

candidates, 25
CHAPTER ONE, 13
integrity in
Leadership,
13
Citizens, 49, 78
civil servants, 16,
26, 28, 33, 49,
53, 68
civil service, 48, 52,
55, 118
common humanity,
65
common sense, 11,
65, 72, 103

Common senses
matters, 5
corruption, 11, 20,
22, 47, 48, 49,
54, 61, 65, 77,
87, 98, 103

D

democracy, 29, 33,
40, 48, 71, 90,
91, 93, 97, 99,
106
democratic culture,
29
desperate
situation, 46
development, 9,
13, 16, 21, 22,
28, 29, 32, 37,
38, 39, 42, 43,
54, 57, 71, 72,
73, 79, 85, 87,
92, 95, 106,
109, 111, 115,
116, 119, 121
director-general,
16
discipline, 11, 17,
32, 47, 68, 83,
87, 88, 112
Discipline, 12, 60

E

economic, 21, 27,
32, 49, 62, 77,
84, 87, 94, 95,
98, 109, 114,
116, 120, 121

Economic
Pragmatism, 6,
11, 113
economy, 38, 46,
49, 61, 93, 114,
115
education tax, 55
election rigging, 14,
20, 22, 91
elections, 20, 21,
29, 38, 91
electoral
malpractices,
20, 29, 91
Embrace Positive
Values, 5, 76
enforcement
agencies, 19,
51, 72
excellence, 15, 18,
34, 88, 115, 118
execution, 24, 57
exploitation, 14,
40, 71

F

Federal
Government, 38
financial controls,
18

G

gangsterism, 8, 69
generation, 31, 39,
78, 114
governance, 9, 11,
17, 19, 27, 34,
40, 52, 64, 66,
85, 94, 96, 107
government
offices, *11*, *13*,
16, *17*, *18*,
19, *20*, *23*,